Blueprint of a
Student Ministry

Blueprint of a Student Ministry

Paul Hudson

Wipf & Stock Publishers
Eugene, Oregon

BLUEPRINT OF A STUDENT MINISTRY

Wipf & Stock Publishers
199 W. 8th Ave., Suite 3
Eugene, OR 97401

ISBN: 1-59752-560-X

Cataloging-in-Publication data:

Hudson, Paul O.

Blueprint of a student ministry / Paul Hudson

p. cm.

Includes bibliographical references.

ISBN 1-59752-560-X

BR128 I54 2006

Manufactured in the U.S.A.

Contents

Blueprint #1

To Remain In Him

To Remain in Him

1. Talk to Me and Not Just About Me! (Spend daily, quality time with Christ)
2. The Ties that Bind (Invest in your spouse and family first)
3. It's a Journal Not a Diary! (Keep a prayer journal)
4. The First and Best Thing (Tithing)
5. A-E-I-O-U (Memorize God's Word)
6. Self Check-out Lanes for Life (Get an accountability partner)

I begin with our relationship with God. To say that it is the most important sounds simple and almost cliché-ish. There are a lot of "most importants" . . . before you go to bed it is most important that you brush your teeth. Putting on clean underwear in the morning is most important. Learning is most important. First impressions are most important. Do you see what I mean? The fact is, there can only be one "most important" and believe me, our relationship with Christ IS the most important. Our relationship with Christ shapes and influences every other relationship we will ever have. How I treat my heavenly Father and God makes a difference in how I treat my wife, my kids, my boss, my parents, my friends, my everyone!

One of the biggest dangers for all of us is that we get to the point where we are talking **about** Him (Christ) more than we are talking **to** Him. When this happens in our ministry, and it can happen, it won't be long until we are running off of fumes and we step out of favor with God. Wouldn't we rather walk in God's favor than have to ask God for a favor? Here is a human example of remaining in Him. PJ and Savannah, my two oldest children, had come outside when I was going to mow the lawn one Saturday morning. Before I could get the mower started they wanted me to chase them and play tag. And we did, for almost an hour. Finally the game of tag ended up in a "tackle daddy" session. It was great. Thirty minutes later as I was cutting the grass, the ice-cream van was driving by with its deafening tunes (that you wake up at night humming). With very little effort needed, I flagged the fellow down. I ran in the house, grabbed PJ and Savannah and hurried them back outside. They were so excited, each knowing immediately what their frozen treat of choice would be. As the ice cream van drove off in a roaring blare, PJ and Savannah both tore open their snacks. Just before PJ took his first bite, he pulled the fudge pop away from his mouth and in a gentle gesture, reached out his little hand toward me and said, "Here, Daddy, you can have the first bite." It was a moment of innocent love and appreciation. He wasn't doing that to hedge himself for the next time the ice cream guy came by. He wasn't doing it out of guilt. He did it because he loved me, which was the same reason I bought it for him to begin with.

Remaining in Him is all about that quality time where you grow your relationship with God. You learn more about Him and yourself. You act and live the way you do because you love God and are thankful to Him for all His goodness. Remaining in Him gives you a thankful heart and an unselfish spirit. You tap into that wellspring of intimate passion of knowing His will for your life and develop the intense burden to share Him with your closest family and the most estranged passer-by. In essence, you spend time with Him in the front yard and because of a healthy relationship, He wants to give you His favor. (Psalm 103:5)

Jesus said, "If a man remains in me and I remain in him, he will bear much fruit." (John 15:5) Then two verses later Jesus says again, "If you remain in me and my words remain in you, ask whatever you wish and it will be given to you." (John 15:7) Remain in Him and your life, your family, and your ministry will be healthy.

1. Talk To Me and Not Just About Me! (Spend daily, quality time with Christ)

To be a true Christ Follower you have to know Him. It is so simple to say yet so hard to practice but until you do your ministry will be built on you. And no matter how great you are in your mind, your opinion doesn't count.

I had a boss who was a true friend one time tell me, "Paul, no matter how great you are, no one is indispensable." What you know can never make up for Who you know. And your creativity, which we will discuss later, will always stem from the one true Creator.

Whether you read the same time each day or even the same place, two things need to be constant: that you give Him your best attention and that you talk honestly with Him. Quality may not be measured in time, but very few things that take "just a few minutes" are really quality! Foster that relationship that you so passionately proclaim to your students.

Three different reasons for reading scripture are:
1. To prepare for Bible study.
2. To stay familiar with God's Word.
3. To get God's thoughts to a life question.

Understand your reason and that will help you determine how and what you should read.

To prepare for a Bible study

When preparing a Bible study you need to know what kind of Bible study it will be. Look at the following types and the ways you can prepare for them.

Topical (life issues type things like dating, love, honesty, friendships, etc...)
1. Pray about the theme and focus.
2. Search a concordance for key words in your theme and focus.

3. Find a key passage to hang the study on.
4. Prayerfully consider the full intent of the key passage, making a couple of talking points.
5. Find additional supporting verses to further solidify your talking points.

Exegetical (verse-by-verse study)

Consider where your students are spiritually and the setting.

1. Choose the section of scripture.
2. Read over it three times to become familiar with it.
3. Use a Bible dictionary, commentaries, and an analytical concordance to study words and phrases.
4. Rewrite verses in your own words to make sure you have a clear understanding and can relate understanding to your students.
5. Make notes accordingly.

Life Example (taking a story from the Bible and relating its truth to everyday life)

1. Choose a story. (Daniel, David, Saul, etc…)
2. Read the passage three times.
3. Pick a central verse.
4. Make notes of the timeline and important details.
5. Prayerfully make talking points that correspond with life issues your students are facing.

Hint: Never plan on using your "Bible Study preparation" time as your intimate time with God. It becomes too easy to focus on what you can tell someone else as opposed to what God is actually telling you.

To stay familiar with God's Word

It is important for every Christian to make God's Word a natural and motivating part of their life. Reading for this purpose will incorporate a little different strategy.

A. Choose a reading plan. Depending on your ability to concentrate, set up a plan that has you read between 15 and 30 minutes each day. There are lots of good reading plans out there to choose from. Lots of Bibles will have reading plans in them.
B. Print out your plan.
C. Follow your plan. (if you miss a day, stay on your plan)

To get God's thoughts to life questions

Each of us encounters times in life when we have questions about life that only God can answer. Finding His plan and His answer to those questions are not only revealed in prayer and through the Holy Spirit but also in His Word.

A. Succinctly write down your question.
B. Be willing to find God's answer instead of looking for scripture to support your personal agenda.
C. Use a concordance to look up key words in your question.
D. Look for characters in the Bible who shared your question.
E. Memorize key verses that answer your question.

2. The Ties that Bind (Invest in your spouse and family first)

After your relationship with God, the next in line of importance is your spouse and your children, and in that order. Your ministry will only be as successful as your marriage. Before you get mad at me for the next statement or disagree, think it through. Your calling to be a student pastor is second to and marked by your calling, privilege, and responsibility to be a husband/wife and father/mother.

If you are not married yet or don't have kids yet, remember that last paragraph but please keep reading.

The problem occurs when we begin to find our fulfillment in "doing our job" rather than in Christ. It can become a quick snare for us all. You experience parents and students who are happy with what is going on at church and you feel affirmed. And that is not wrong. It becomes a snare when you make that affirmation your motivation. The affirmation should be just that . . . affirmation. Remember, you will teach students by the events you don't attend as much as by the ones you do attend. When they see you putting your spouse first, you are teaching them God's plan for marriage that many of them never see at home.

I will admit there are seasons in life. There are times of the year when you are out more and have more serious time crunches. But family must always come first. Think of it this way. Christy, my wonderful wife, and I had PJ and Savannah and waited nearly 5 years to have our third child, Aubrey. After Aubrey was born, Savannah, reeling with the middle child syndrome, promptly announced in a matter of fact tone, "We love Aubrey the most, don't we Daddy!" I replied that we love each of them the same and then asked her why she thought that. Savannah's 5 year old brain had equated the amount of personal attention given to Aubrey at the fragile stage of her life to loving her more. I quickly explained that we didn't love her more but that she just needed us more right now.

Some of us in error take this approach to our ministry. While you are to love what you do, feel called to what you do, and receive energy from what you do, no where does it say that it takes a lateral position to your family. Get this one concept down and it has been worth the price of this book ten times over. Your relationship with Jesus affects every other relationship you will have, be it professional or otherwise. And so will your relationship with your spouse. How you treat him/her, touch him/her, and take care of him/her will help keep you pure and passionate or push you into rebellion against God.

There is lots of expertise in this field and I don't want to show my ignorance by going on and on. However, I encourage you to take note of some worthy thoughts that may help you keep your family first:

1. Always talk to your spouse before you commit to an event or engagement.
2. Take your days off.
3. Go AWAY on vacation.
4. Have a set date night.
5. Be sweet and tender with him/her in front of your students.
6. Take your spouse with you as much as you can.
7. Don't use your children as an excuse.

8. Help your kids see God as good and not a task-master.
9. Spend time with your kids everyday.
10. Spend individual time with your kids weekly.

My desire is that PJ, Savannah, and Aubrey get through high school and say that living in the home of a Student Pastor was great! And please know that God will teach you things about His love through your children and they need your love more than you could ever imagine.

3. It's a Journal Not a Diary! (Keep a prayer journal)

Depending on your personality, this may not be easy but it will certainly pay off. I struggle with my attention span and remembering what God has done in my life as much as just a week ago. So keeping a prayer journal allows me to slow down and collect my thoughts to God. A prayer journal is a great way to keep from speeding through your prayer time.

I have been through times where I write every day and then times where I only make entries once a month. Somewhere in the middle is where I have landed. Once every couple of days keeps me from being legalistic about writing but affords me the chance to read what I have prayed for in the very recent past. Find what works for you but remember that honesty has to be first place. I keep my journal as a collection of letters to my God.

4. The First and Best Thing (Tithing)

Sometimes, as church workers we adopt the mentality that the church owes us something. That "something" is easily defined as money and the temptation is to become less than scrupulous with our own giving. But don't be fooled, the responsibility and privilege to tithe is not held succinctly for the lay person. Tithing is a spiritual act of worship and to avoid or excuse yourself from it is to hold back from God.

A. Write a check for your tithe. Do not take it out of any reimbursements the church may owe you.

B. Make your tithe check the first check you write after depositing your pay check.
C. Tithe on your gross.

5. A-E-I-O-U (Memorize God's Word)

Do you recognize A, E, I, O, and U? Of course you do. They are the vowels of the English alphabet. And how do you know that? Because at age 5 or 6 you had those five little letters drilled, hammered, and etched in your head. Those five simple letters are the forming blocks of all you speak and read today. They are vitally important to your ability to communicate. And so is God's Word. Memorizing scripture is like crafting God's mind into your own mountain of thoughts. To personalize His values and standards is to assure sincerity and authenticity. Consider the following benefits of memorizing scripture:

- It improves your memory.
- It improves your speaking ability.
- It gives you ammunition in spiritual warfare. (Eph 6)
- It helps you fight sinful temptation. (2 Corinthians 10:13)
- It gives guidance in tense situations. (John 17:17)
- It draws you closer to the heart of God. (Ps 119:105)

Here are just a few suggestions for scripture memorization that will keep it fresh:

- Memorize with your family and work on it daily.
- Memorize with your small group or selected group of students.
- Work on 4-10 verse sections per semester.
- Have selected portions to memorize for special events.

6. Self Check-out Lanes for Life (Get an accountability partner)

So here I am standing in the longest line ever formed since the creation of mankind at Wal-Mart. I am running late for my kid's program and all I have is one stinking item. I jockey for position in the line next to me and then fly between lanes looking for the fastest moving one but each solemn row seems to inch along at a pace only a snail could appreciate. Out of the corner of my eye, "Eureka!" Like gold to a weary miner, I spot a line that is moving at a blistering speed (at this point blistering has become greatly relative). I zoom to the end of the check-outs and there it is, a self-check-out stand. My attention was heightened as I neared my turn in line. Drag the sticker with the long lines and numbers past the red beam of light thingy until it goes "beep" and I'm on my way. It's simple! No problem. But wait, what is this? The lady at the desk near the self-check, what is she doing? And then I realized, she is the checker for the self-checkout station. Every time there is a problem she is Johnny—or rather Joanne—on the spot to make sure you are scanning, bagging, and paying correctly. As I helped myself through my first self-check out experience, apparently it was not so "self" oriented. I had a problem with the bagging and as for the paying part, I will always remember coins first.

Much like the Wal-Mart self-check out stands, being accountable to yourself may sound good but the practicality of it isn't the best. Especially when it comes to holding yourself accountable to acting justly, loving mercy, and walking humbly with God. (Micah 6:8) But the idea of having someone hold you accountable for your actions, thoughts, and words can be a trifle scary but also amazingly liberating. Scary, because someone else will know your shortcomings. Liberating because you know you will do better when someone is watching. Each of us knows what it is to falter on a New Year's resolution, to mess up, and to quit. But that should not be the norm or even acceptable. Each January millions of people make resolutions that don't last as long as it would take to finish a box of Hostess Ding Dongs. (My favorite from when I was a boy. You know the kind that came wrapped in foil. A glass of ice cold milk and a couple of Ding Dongs and life was good.) They have a plan, an idea, and the desire but what they don't have is accountability. A person who will make them face their commitment; someone who cares if they succeed as much as they themselves care. There is some measure of pain, loss, or embarrassment that accountability parades directly in front of us as to not allow us to forget, slide, or settle. Accountability is the key to change and the key to consistency. Without it, we are creatures bound by the depths of our own selfishness. Paul said that even those things I don't want to do, I find myself doing. And those things I wish I would do, I don't. (Romans 7:15-16) Why? Because left to its own, our flesh is weak and shallow.

So how does an accountability partner work?

1. Get a partner or two. Prayerfully consider someone who you could share growing spiritual with. He/She should be the same sex as you and near your age. Your spouse should be your greatest friend, spiritual partner, lover, and confidante . . . but not your accountability partner. Trust me, there will be accountability with your spouse but this is different. This will be someone you can talk over life issues with that can bring a fresh perspective to the table.

2. Write a set of accountability questions. Take some time to think about what areas of your life need the most accountability. Most of the time there are four major areas; our walk with God, our relationship with our wife and kids, our finances, and our weaknesses.

3. Meet regularly. Whether it is once a week or once a month, set a time to meet regularly. Have a protocol in place for what events are worth missing accountability time for. (vacation, sickness, etc)

Blueprint #2

To Build Community

"Now you are the body of Christ, and each one of you is a part of it."
1 Corinthians 12:27

To Build Community
1. Hey, That's Us! (Create an identity)
2. In MY House? (Regularly invite students to your home)
3. Speak into the Mic! (Give students opportunity to share their testimony)
4. Calendar Up! (Create a monthly calendar)
5. I Read You Loud and Clear! (Create a monthly newsletter or other form of communication)
6. Say "Cheese!" (Put up pictures from youth events)
7. The Ultimate Fan (Go to students' sporting events)
8. Ad Effects (Advertise in school publications)
9. More than a Song and Dance! (Get students to sing and play at youth services)
10. No Shirt! No Shoes! No Service! (Use clothing to build bonds)

Building community is the process of growing together as a family through life experiences. It is one of the fundamental building blocks of the church, yet many times we try to fashion a youth program on loud music, edgy programs, and wicked bad lights rather than relationships. Jesus said He would draw all men unto Himself (John 12:32) not to a program. Paul wrote in Acts 2:42 "they were all together and had everything in common". This idea of being family is bigger than what we give it credit. Maybe it is because we come from busted families, deal with parents going through divorce, and hurt along side students who are dealing with single parent living situations. But for whatever the reason, we have become numb to the intrinsic need for family, the need that God gave us and Jesus fulfilled. In Jesus we are His brothers and sisters (Matthew 3:35) and God's children (John 1:12, Romans 8:16, 1 John 3:1). Family implies a sense of belonging, love, and loyalty. If you are not harboring, protecting, and growing a sense of family and community in your youth group, you will fight against the selfishness in students rather than instill in them the joy of belonging.

1. Hey, That's Us! (Create an identity)

Okay, a cool name or logo is what you are looking for, and that's great. But before you get there you need to understand three principles.

1. Give your greatest and best efforts to God. He desires for you to consistently apply your very best to everything you do in your ministry. Defining **who** you are as a body and **what** your purpose is should rate your very best efforts as well.
2. Your identity should be found in Christ. If your identity is not found in Christ, you will become a casualty of fad and fashion wars. Knowing that who you are is wrapped up in your relationship with God will help bring focus to your search for a name.
3. Your logo and name should be a tool. In a positive way, use your name and logo to create awareness and presence in your community.

One of the first and best things you can do to help build community among your students is to create a youth group identity - who you are, what your focus and goals are, and what you are about. You want your students and their friends to be able to hear a word or see a logo and immediately feel a part of something bigger than their individuality. That something bigger is family, it's community, and it grows synergy. As much as they want to be themselves, they have a deep desire and need to feel a sense of belonging and unity. A couple of questions that will help you in discovering your identity are:

- What is your purpose? Formalize it in a statement. You can begin by sketching out ideas with leadership students.
- What is the vision for your youth ministry? Who do you envision reaching and how do you see yourself reaching them?
- What do you want to be known for or who do you want to be known as?

Give yourself a name other than First Baptist Youth or First United Methodist Youth. Show more creativity and purpose in naming yourself. Begin by brainstorming names that would encompass your purpose and your vision. Compile a list of companies, logos, web slang, and any other creative words or names you like. Then bring the core group of your student body into the process to help make the final decision. Their participation will show you just how much ownership they will take in the youth group.

The tie that binds all this together is the spiritual connection your name has to your purpose statement. (Hint: the more you have to explain a name or logo, the less effective it will be.) You want something that is so dynamic and so obvious that any student can grasp the connection. Obvious does not mean simple or plain, it just means obvious. And you want to make sure and tie in with the church as a whole. Do NOT disassociate yourself from the body of the church. You will do yourself and your students harm.

2. In MY House? (Regularly invite students to your home)

Get students into your home. Now don't get me wrong, this is not an open invitation to show up anytime. We all know with the schedules of teens that could be disaster. However, having a set day each week or month for your students to come to your house can be beneficial. For the sake of your family, make it convenient for you first. Then, establish a beginning and ending time. There will of course be those times that one or two want to stay late to talk about serious things, but as a rule set a leaving time.

The purpose is for them to see you being a normal person. And this brings me to three warnings . . .

1. Never watch or listen to anything that falls out of the boundaries of Ephesians 5:1-3.
2. NEVER be alone with someone of the opposite sex at your house.
3. Don't force a Bible study. Chances are that from time to time they will bring up Biblical or moral questions. You can then take time in a living room setting to answer them. But part of growing together is being yourselves together.

This should be a relationship building time where they get to know you and your family and enjoy just being together in a healthy environment.

3. Speak into the Mic! (Give students opportunity to share their testimony)

Allowing students to share what God is doing in their lives is vital. It accomplishes two goals:

1. It gives that student a venue to express his/her heart.
2. It shows other students that God is moving around them.

Not everyone will feel comfortable sharing and that is fine. And you don't want the same two or three doing it all the time either. A healthy mixture of guys and girls and at different events will keep it fresh and real. The idea is for it to not come across as forced or canned. It needs to be genuine and sincere.

4. Calendar Up! (Create a monthly calendar)

I know it sounds simple but it is so important. If it is done with a little creativity and some flare it will pay big dividends. It will cause your students to see themselves in the bigger picture of your youth group when you make a youth group calendar with all the youth events labeled. Do your best to make it large and hang it in a place where every student will see it. You can also make smaller copies that students can hang in their room, in their locker, or on their refrigerator. You can even put in on your web site. The following are some things you want to make sure and put on the calendar.

- Birthdays (students and workers)
- Sunday schedules
- Wednesday schedules
- Special events
- Meetings
- Practices

5. I Read You Loud and Clear! (Create a monthly newsletter or other form of communication)

When you publish anything, remember who the audience is when you make the final edit. Done well, a youth group newsletter should answer two questions:

1. What is going on?
2. Where can I fit in?

The first question covers events and games. Collect pictures from parents of sporting events, recitals, and drama events on a weekly or monthly basis to use in the newsletter. You should strive to cover a wide variety of events and make sure and touch each segment of your student population. Whether they admit it or not, students like to see themselves in pictures.

The second question is answered by showing events and opportunities directly involved with your youth program. Inundate them with information about how and where to plug in.

Quick note: keep it fresh. Take a look at the magazines they are reading, (especially the ones you wish they weren't) and you will get a good example of what is catching their eye and their attention. Do your best to make it as first-class as possible. Remember that they handle change very well.

6. Say "Cheese!" (Put up pictures from youth events)

The bottom line here is that you begin and maintain a collection of your students in action. The following are some suggestions for getting pictures.

1. Designate a student to take pictures at each event.
2. Ask parents for pictures.
3. Purchase a camera just for youth photos.
4. Buy disposable cameras for big group events. Pass them out and collect them at the end of the event.
5. Ask a parent to come in with their camera once a month to take photos.

Whether you put up regular 5X7 pictures on the mirrors in the bathroom or hang huge eight foot wall pictures, your students enjoy seeing themselves and others having fun. Pictures cause them to remember good times, to associate with other students, and to feel connected. Make sure you have a good mix and change them out regularly and the bigger the better.

So how do I display them?

Often times we will use the same pictures in our youth room for almost three weeks, but we change their location weekly. The following are some tips for the kind of pictures you are looking for.

1. Pictures of a small group of close friends in a pose, smiling or playing around.
2. Shots of games and funny activities where they are involved.
3. Large group photos of worship and movement. (Pictures of them sitting still watching you are good to have to put in a parent newsletter but not for the walls.)

As often as you can, put the event logo or tag onto the picture.

So how do I print them?

You can print color pictures on your desk jet but we all know its quality is not so good. Try some of the following:

1. Make a deal with a local print house to make 5 or 10 or 20 poster sized photos for you each month and budget for them.
2. Use a color copier to make various sized pictures.
3. Invest in a plotter. *A plotter is a huge printer that will print in widths of 36 to 60 inches wide and however long you wish. With a plotter you can tile projects to build complete back drops, make your own posters, and even print pictures to cover a wall. You can check the web for plotters but we use an HP and have found it to be adequate. And the price? You can expect to pay somewhere between $2,500 and $12,000 depending on the size and quality of the machine you purchase.

7. The Ultimate Fan (Go to students' sporting events)

There are two aspects of going to youth sporting events. One is to make contact with parents and the other is to be a real part of that student's life. When you are there you become a part of that life experience with them. As you cheer and holler with their parents your ministry is woven into their family history. You build greater influence with both that student and their parents. Whether it is a football game, a band concert, or a school play, be involved.

You cannot attend every game, recital, or school play. Do your best to invest in students and not school programs. By this I mean attend events and participate in functions that will help build relationships with students. The following are some ideas for investing in students through school activities.

A. Purchase season tickets to all the schools where you have students. Make a place for this in your youth budget. It is as important as any resource you might buy from the bookstore. *Check with the athletic departments, some high school districts give passes to student pastors.*

B. Talk to parents to see where they will be sitting so you can sit with them. It seems much more intentional when you have called or talked to the parents before hand. Once you have committed to be there, don't fail them.

C. Carry church cards or youth group promo with you. Don't force the conversation to church stuff but many times it will go there so be prepared.

D. Watch the game. Nothing will frustrate a parent faster than if you are talking when their kid scores.

E. Try to talk to the student or students after the game if only to say "good game". You want to be encouraging and not just to be seen.

F. Wear school clothing. It makes people feel you are a part or have gone the extra mile. It looks like you planned to be there instead of just happened by.

G. Be on time or early to games. They will be glad you are there no matter when you show up, but being there on time means it is important to you.

8. Ad Effects (Advertise in school publications)

Advertising will always cost money. The trick is to determine which method will give you the most exposure for your target. Sometimes your target is parents and sometimes your target is students. You have to know the difference and make the ads fit accordingly. You can expect to spend between $50 and $500 per ad venture.

You are advertising your youth group's identity and your church name. It is good to use your logo at every opportunity. If you need help creating a logo and identity there are several good companies who, for a fee, can help you build an identity based on your purpose statement just for your group.

When advertising it is always best to have a game plan before you start. For instance, in one year you may purchase one year book ad, one football program ad, and two calendar ads. Then the next year, change up schools and advertising avenues. Hint: advertise heaviest where you have the most participation.

Here are some creative ways to get your youth group's name into your schools.

Free:

1. Be a substitute teacher.
2. Wear a youth group shirt to school lunches.
3. Announce games.
4. Make banners and posters for outfields, fences, and press boxes.
5. Volunteer to help clean up after games.
6. Work the concession stand.

Not-So-Free:

1. Take out a page to congratulate the seniors in the year book.
2. Purchase an ad on sports calendars.
3. Purchase a fence ad for the softball or baseball team.
4. Purchase a "GO Team" ad in the football program.
5. Sponsor half-time pizza give-a-way at basketball games.
6. Sponsor a water table at a track event.
7. Pass out footballs with your logo in the team's colors.
8. Have seat cushions made with your logo and team's color.
9. Make the big paper thingy the football players run through.
10. Purchase Gatorade for the team.
11. Purchase water bottles for the team with your logo on them.

9. More than a Song and Dance! (Get students to sing and play at youth services)

Whether it is a youth choir of 100, a solo, or anything in between, getting your students involved in the actual body of your youth services will grow community. They will begin to see themselves as a part of the worship and not a spectator of the service. There are so many ways to use students. Student participation makes the service "theirs" and not just "yours". Of course there should be guidelines but the underlying premise is to involve students.

I would not worry about ability as much as stability. The heart and character of the person on stage will shine much longer and farther than his/her talent. Our praise band has Bible study together and accountability partners. Taking your students from the seat to the stage also brings to them added responsibility. One of our verses has become Ps 51:17, "The sacrifices of God are a broken spirit!"

Here are some ways your students can be involved.

1. They can sing in a praise band.
2. They can act or help with props for a drama team.
3. They can pray at the beginning and end of meetings.
4. They can run Power Point.
5. They can help set up the stage before services.
6. They can run the CD player.
7. They can sing, play, or sign special music.
8. They can make the announcements.
9. They can be door greeters.

The best advice in this area would be to make sure you set them up to succeed. While a student is singing make sure you are paying attention. If you ask a student to run the sound board or PPT, let them do it. Even through mistakes you will teach them and they will grow to trust in your leadership.

Five tips for vocalists and instrumentalists:

1. Give them their music in advance. For instrumentalists, mail them their sheet music before you plan to practice it for the first time together. For vocalists, get them copies of the music on CD. Always make extras.
2. Have designated practices that are mandatory. You teach them responsibility if you institute a policy that if they don't practice, they don't play. Any exception only implies that your youth group service is not worth the best. I have found that the more I strive for authenticity and perfection in this area, the more committed the students are to the team.
3. Let them sing and perform music they enjoy. You really need to be a student of students. Learn what kind of music your students are in to. Then try revamping hymns and always be on the look out for new worship music.
4. Keep the arrangements on their level.

5. Find someone to work with them who knows more than they do. Music will rise to the level and ability of the leader.

10. No Shirt! No Shoes! No Service! (Use clothing to build bonds)

Clothing with your youth group's name and logo reaches beyond your doors and shouts the concept of family even when you aren't around. The clothing has to be relevant to today's styles and fashionably modest. Check out the latest styles at Old Navy and Abercrombie to see what your students are wearing. Look for simple designs that can be easily and cheaply recreated. Incorporate those styles of shirts into mission trip themes, Bible study series, and generic youth group logo shirts.

T-shirts are not fundraisers and you will always either have way too many or not nearly enough. So make sure you budget for them. As far as the design, every person's taste is different. I prefer to either design my own or allow my local printer to create something for me based on the concept I give her.

Here are a few simple rules I try to follow when it comes to clothing.

1. Show samples to a core group of students before making a big order.
2. Order the right sizes.
3. The 5-10 rule. I try to purchase most of our clothing at under $5 or under $10 so I can charge either $5 or $10. This means you work with your printer to compare costs of 1 color, 2 color, 3 color, full front, or back pricing.
4. Give some of it away. I try to give a few shirts away each time to different students and to ones who will wear them and represent us well.

Random thoughts about clothing:

1. Have a T-Shirt Day during the week where your students wear a youth group t-shirt to school that day. Your students will have fun and other students will ask questions.
2. Use extra shirts as give-a-ways to first time visitors.
3. Make a display with each new t-shirt you have.

4. Have your praise band promo the shirts the week before or the week that they go on sale.
5. Display all the shirts you have ever had somewhere in your youth room.
6. Do whatever it takes to get them in the hands or on the backs of your student leaders.

Conclusion

Your students need to see themselves as a part of a small group, the youth group, and the church as a whole. Every student needs to belong. And small group is where a student will really belong. Whether in the form of a Sunday morning Bible study or mid-week accountability group, the first level of community is found in a small group. In a small group you are missed, thought of, and prayed for. While your students will enjoy the atmosphere of a big crowd, they also have a need for intimacy only found in small group. They will cry together, laugh together, and solve life problems together.

And not only do they need to feel a belonging but they all want to belong on the winning team. Your youth group should be **the** "winning team" in your students' minds. Do your best to offer first class parties, Bible studies, and events and they will consider the youth group to be first class. Youth group is where your students will find their *next* level of family and intimacy.

Blueprint #3

To Build Relationships

To Build Relationships
1. Ala Carte (Eat lunch at schools)
2. The Big Hello (Talk to every person present)
3. Make Mention Often (Pray for your students every day)
4. The Ministry of "Hang" (Find time to just hang out with them)
5. Handwritten Notes (Write your students personal notes)
6. The Mini Me Approach (Mentor someone or a group of someones)
7. Happy Birthday, Harry! (Contact students on their birthdays)
8. Knock, Knock! Who's There? (Make home visits for big life events – birthdays, family deaths, broken legs, etc.)

The life and maturity of your ministry is built upon relationships. Your relationship to God, to your wife and kids, to students, to parents, to teachers and school officials, to your pastor, and the list goes on. Relationships build connecting points between people, ideas, and convictions. And connecting with people is your ministry. Communication in and of itself is not connecting but at every level of connecting, there is some form of communication. This chapter deals with ways to connect and build relationships with students.

So why is connecting so important? Imagine that you have spent hours putting together a 1000 piece puzzle. With tenacity and precision you have not left your post until all 1000 pieces found their proper spot. In near mental exhaustion you stand up to soak in the full breadth of your labor. As you are standing, your shirt catches the corner piece and without any extra effort, all of a sudden pieces are falling off everywhere. That tingling sensation of blood rushing to your ears and face comes over you as you desperately search for words while at the same time biting your tongue. The pieces were fitted but not connected. In student ministry it is not enough to just fit students into a spot, they must be connected. If you wanted to be able to keep each piece connected, you would have to use puzzle glue or sticky paper or something that has adhesive, something that will hold them together. In a youth group, that **something** is being connected in relationships.

Every student that comes into your ministry is another important piece of your ministry puzzle. When students attend an event or program, sign up for a camp, retreat, or small group, they are in essence joining their piece to the bigger part of the puzzle. But they are not really connected until there is a relationship built. Relationships are the adhesive for your ministry puzzle because relationships are what keep people connected. Although their stepping inside your four walls is what joins them to your ministry, the connection usually requires you to step outside your four walls to maintain the relationship: attend games, recitals, school lunches, and so on. In your ministry, students and workers alike will make commitments to programs. They will commit to study, to be on time, to show up and lead or follow. But what solidifies that commitment and makes it a reality is not the program. The program is a tool. The true commitment is to relationships.

So how do we build relationships in our ministry that are genuine, true, and meaningful enough for a student to buy in to? Here are eight simple ideas you can incorporate or reinvent to suit your ministry. The key is that it takes more than eye contact to make a real connection and each one of your leaders (students and adults) needs to buy into the idea of being family by growing relationships. They need to be puzzle builders.

1. A La Carte (Eat lunch at schools)

In honesty I admit that this tactic can be intimidating for any student pastor, but in the end it is highly rewarding. It is like getting your teeth cleaned. You are so nervous before you go but once you get there, it's not too bad and the end result is great. Every student pastor knows the awkwardness of standing in a school hallway as an outsider, especially if you are over 30. Students bounce off of you as if you were a human locker, flooding your brain with memories of your first few days of junior high, and concerned teachers give you the stare of death. Who are you and what are you up to?! But in knowing that you are called to be their pastor and called to build relationships, you can find your strength in God.

Here are some simple guidelines for eating lunch at schools:

1. Get permission. Either call or stop by the school office and get permission from the appropriate personnel, usually the principal. More often than not, they are glad to have you on their campus but it shows respect and willingness to follow the rules.

2. Respect teachers. Never put yourself in a compromising position where it is you and the students against the teachers. It is not healthy for the students or your job.

3. Check-in. Most every school today has a "visitor check-in policy". Know it and abide by it.

4. Let your students know you are coming and when you aren't. By telling them the Sunday or Wednesday before that you are coming, they will be ready for you. Many times they will save you a seat and ask unchurched friends to sit with them.

5. Give students your attention. Many times a well meaning teacher can absorb your attention away from your main purpose. Tell teachers that you will stop back by on your way out, and then do your best to give your whole attention to each student as you talk to them.

6. Change up your visit patterns. Sometimes I will sit for a whole lunch period with one student or one group of students. Other times I will walk around the lunch room, talking to every student I know until that lunch period is over. Both patterns are important and serve a specific purpose. Sitting with one student or group of students allows you to really build relationships. You may have

to tell other students that you will sit with their group next week and then you can give them your full attention. The benefit of walking and talking is that you get to meet new students and it is relatively easy to communicate at that level. "Hey John, how are you man!? I prayed for you today. How is your mom, dad, sister, etc? Don't forget about tomorrow night . . . it is Wednesday!"

7. Every Monday! You have to do what works for you and your ministry, but I have found that going to the same school on the same day each week is optimal. The students get to where they expect you and you are certainly more consistent than if you were to just hit and miss visit. You also become part of the students' and teachers' pattern for that day. Their perception is that you are there all the time. And that is a good thing.

*I rarely actually eat so that I can have more talking time. But if you have a special liking to cafeteria style gourmet food, dig in, Skipper.

2. The Big Hello (Talk to every person present)

Students at times can wear their feelings on their sleeves. Making sure you speak to every student that steps through the doors will let them know you care. There will be needy students, new students, and situations that beg for your more intimate attention but as a standard talk to every student. Knowing what to say is secondary to actually talking. Pray for wisdom and guidance but be brave and lead by example. If you are in a "fly by" mode where you have a limited amount of time to get by to every student, shake their hand, give a side hug, or put your hand on their shoulder, call them by name, and tell them you are glad they are there. Follow that up with a comment about what's coming up that event or with a comment about an upcoming event. By making eye contact and calling them by name you have made a personal connection. In a few short words about the event or upcoming event you have made a social connection. And in the way you touch a student, you can make an emotional connection.

In the "slow down" mode you will take time to ask students open ended questions. Try to talk with students who you don't get to spend a lot of time with. Often times, while in this mode, there will be needy students who sense your lack of urgency and try to consume your time. Handle that by quietly reminding them you get to see or talk to them often and that there are some visitors or fringe students who you really need to talk with.

There are four benefits from the Big Hello:

1. You get to know students and remember their names.
2. The students know you care. When you stand before them you are not *that* guy (that guy who leads the students), you are *the* guy (the guy who is their student pastor and who talks to them, knows them and prays for them).
3. Fewer students fall through relationship cracks.
4. It examples good leadership for your student leaders and adults. It teaches them to step away from the easy conversations and do ministry.

3. Make Mention Often (Pray for your students every day)

"We always thank God for all of you, mentioning you in our prayers." 1 *Thessalonians 1:2*

In every letter Paul wrote, he encouraged his family in God by letting them know he prayed for them. And I believe this was more than a formal greeting at the beginning of a letter. I believe it was the sincere love Paul had for these people that so filled his heart to remember them in prayer. It is a chance for you to take students' needs and desires and life before the Creator and Author of life to ask favor for them. At the heart of this action or practice must be love. Paul wrote that the only thing that matters is faith expressing itself in love. (Galatians 5:6) You speaking to God is faith and you speaking to God on their behalf is love. If you pray for your student just to say you have done it you have missed the mark. The following is what has worked best for me.

1. Write each person's name on a card. Writing their name helps you remember them. Several times there has been a visitor come and I put their name in my prayer file on a card with all the others. I begin praying for that student and every time I do I see their face. When they come back in a month, I remember their name. That really gets their attention. Many times I have even had parents

I didn't know call me and tell me their students really enjoyed our youth group and couldn't believe I remembered their names. Praying for your students daily will help you know them.

2. Mark their card daily. As you pray for your students, make a mark beside their name. I don't usually put the date. Normally I put an "X" or a check to signify that I prayed for them. Sometimes I pray scripture for them and will write the reference on the card. I also put special words of encouragement at times on the back of the card or along the sides.

3. Mail them the card. At the end of a month or two I will make up a form letter that explains the checks and scripture references. I mail each student the letter along with their card.

There are two sides to praying for your students. Talking to God and talking to them. Talking to God - Make sure you actually pray for them. Pour out your heart to God for your students and earnestly pray for them by name. Putting their names on cards helped me from hurriedly running down a list of names.

Talking to them - Let them know you prayed for them. Be careful not to sound braggadocios. If you pray for them in humility and sincerity, it will be easy to tell them you prayed for them with humility and sincerity. James 5:16 says, "The prayer of a righteous man is powerful and effective."

Your earnest prayer will bring about ***life change*** and your letting them know you are praying for them brings about ***relationship change***.

Other ways to pray for your students are:

1. Pray for 20 students (or a percentage of your students) a day.
2. Have a master list and read over their names.
3. Pray for the big events in their lives (games, recitals, tests, graduation, etc...)
4. Print up scripture cards with blanks for students' names. Pray through the scripture on the card, writing their name in the blanks. Then mail them the card.
5. Have prayer lists made up. (Divide them by grade, sports teams, activities, clubs, etc...) And pray for a list each day.

*Besides praying for students as God brings them to my heart and head, I will pray for all my students on days I am in the office. The reason I do it is because prayer really does make a difference. Not just telling them I'm praying . . . but actually praying for them makes the difference.

4. The Ministry of "Hang" (Find time to just hang out with them)

So what does it mean to "hang" and where in the world did that phrase come from? Actually, it was coined during the late 60's when people were finding ways to rebel against anything and everything. By the droves adventurous teens lined the sides of the bridges near Woodstock farm and dangled their feet off the edge. And thus was born the phrase "just hang'n". Okay, so that's hog wash. Actually it is a surfing term originating from a reference to a move where someone dangles their toes off the front edge of the board. Regardless, in our society it means simply, doing nothing . . . together. It is the favored past time of the uncreative or overactive student. Just hanging means there has to be no plan, no schedule but certainly implies that whatever happens should be fun.

The trick to "hanging" with your students is to leave the time wide open for whatever but keeping parameters that help teach responsibility.
1. Pick a place that is easily accessible and not offensive to parents.
2. Choose a time that does not conflict with parental parameters.
3. Always give supervision.

5. Handwritten Notes (Write your students personal notes)

When my wife and I got married we were putting all our stuff together and I came across a big box of letters. "What is this?" I asked. They were every birthday card, sweet note, letter, and announcement she ever received. And the same is probably true of most of us. We have saved encouraging letters and notes and even those little scribbled pieces of notebook paper from someone special. In an age of e-mails, quick link, and online instant messaging, handwritten notes are still supreme. Which is more meaningful to you? The birthday card you receive that barely has a name scribbled near the closing of the manufactured witty saying or the card that has a note personally written on the blank page. Most of us don't even take time to read the manufactured print. We just look for the cash.

This practice has meant so much to my ministry and has been so successful that I even have special note cards printed. Here are some random thoughts about writing notes:

1. Always write their name. Often times I will use the nickname I have given them. This is yet another connecting point. (I write their real name on the envelope.)
2. Keep it fairly short. Don't write two pages front and back.
3. Let them know you are praying for them.
4. Encourage them to spend time with Jesus.
5. Never write rebuke or discipline in a letter, only words of encouragement. Rebuke and correction are meant for eye-to-eye meetings. Writing your rebuke, frustration, or correction is an easy way out and it doesn't usually work. Not to mention that letter is then held as ammunition.
6. Give a scripture reference for them to look up and read. Not the same one every time either.

6. The Mini Me Approach (Mentor someone or a group of someones)

Pouring your life into a student or small group of students will bring about a huge impact in your ministry. You will build close friendships with those students. Yes, you will have to hurt, cry, play, laugh, and live with them, but you will also be raising up leaders and equipping them to live a life that pleases God. In turn, those students will affect other students in a positive way.

There are four steps to effective mentoring:

1. Example life, love, and leadership. You have to spend enough time with them so they can see how God living in you helps you to handle different aspects of your life.
2. Accountability. Being a mentor without any accountability is just being friends. Set up accountability questions that cover several areas of their life: home, school, friends, music, habits, dating, etc...

3. Spend time in God's Word. Together you have to use God's Word to answer life questions and to grow. Without God's Word, all you have is a little club.
4. Invest in their life. You have to take one-on-one time with them to talk about what God is doing in their life. Help them see what they are missing and what they are getting exactly right. Be more of an encourager than a rebuker.

My small group of guys is very close to each other, to me and to my family. They are the guys I turn to for leadership in our youth group. They lead out in prayer. They organize events. They are in charge of lead teams like praise band, tech team, outreach, and much more. The reason they do that is because they are growing and maturing as followers of Christ.

*Note: be careful not to make "teacher's pets". This will cause students to feel left out and even betrayed. Do your best to keep the playing field level by giving attention, as best you can, in equal amounts.

7. Happy Birthday, Harry! (Contact students on their birthdays)

This is very simple but meaningful (otherwise it wouldn't have made it to this list). If you think about it, the people who contact you on your birthday are usually those closest to you. By calling or talking to your student on their birthday, you gain a trust and closeness. You step into that circle of friends that remembered, cared, and celebrated.

Here are some ways you can contact them on their birthday:
1. Call them. Try first thing in the morning, unless it is summer then maybe sometime after noon would be better.
2. Send birthday card. Write a personal note inside!! Ha ha
3. Run by their house. You can talk to them, drop off a gift on the front porch, or leave a note on the door.
4. E-mail.
5. The Pink Flamingo. Use a pink flamingo or some other yard ornament that you can move around from yard to yard on students' birthdays.

*We also put students' birthdays on our wall calendar in the youth room and on the calendar in our monthly student newsletter.

8. Knock, Knock! Who's There? (Make home visits for big life events - birthdays, family deaths, broken legs, etc...)

Make a phone call before you drop by, but a home visit always communicates that you care. Depending on the size of your ministry, home visits may not be an option all the time, but reserving them for big life events keeps them special. Here are some general home-visit guidelines:

1. Only go inside when invited.
2. Only go inside when a parent or guardian is home.
3. Try to keep the visit to about 10 minutes.
4. Pray with your student and/or his/her parents before you leave.
5. Be respectful of property and privacy.

If you remain in God, give community building opportunities, and foster healthy environments for building strong, God-centered relationships, you will be successful. Develop your relationship building skills by grafting these eight simple concepts into your ministry plan. For success is where God's faithfulness is met with your obedience to bring about life change.

Blueprint #4

To Stay Organized

"For God is not a God of disorder but of peace."
1 Corinthians 14:33

To Stay Organized
1. By the Numbers (Make "to do" lists everyday)
2. My People Will Get with Your People (Keep a calendar)
3. No More Wing and a Prayer Services (Plan Bible studies in advance)
4. Under "C" for Christmas! (Make folders and notebooks for each event, series, and program)
5. Bueller? Bueller? (Keep attendance records)
6. The Three "Ables" (Set identifiable, quantifiable, and attainable goals)
7. August to July (Plan a year at a time)

Why is it that the position of the student pastor is so many times looked at with little respect and lack of appreciation? Don't the collective "they" know how hard it is to stay abreast of the societal ebb and flow while at the same time fostering spiritual aptitude in a generation marked by cultish fads and technological genius? For the most part ***no***, they don't. But our effort or determination is not on trial, so quit whining. Most frequently it is our personal self disciplines that are called to task. Your ability to **organize** your life and your ministry will **shape** your life and ministry. I have found personally, the more organized my life is, the clearer my vision, the more focused my mission, and the more fun my passion.

Truth be told, most student pastors lack organizational skills to purposefully get through a week much less a semester or year. What I propose is that you plan tentatively for a year, plan directly for a month and plan extensively for a week. The following is a list of seven acts to help you stay organized.

1. By the Numbers (Make "to do" lists everyday)

As you have probably surmised by this point, I like lists. I am comfortable with lists. Lists are my friend and they can be your friend, too. Working off of a list is a simple way to organize your thoughts and your daily plans. You don't want to be legalistic about your life, but you do want to be effective. I treat "to do" lists as a way of organizing and managing my time. The "list" as I call it, is a tool. Don't be confused, the list is not your goals. It is what is necessary to accomplish your goals for that day, week, and year. Setting your goals will be discussed in number six of this chapter. Here are some thoughts as you consider making your list.

1. Take time each day to work on your list. Making the list is not your "end." It is the means to the end. So make a habit of collecting your "to do list" items in a central spot. Use a PDA, a notepad, a napkin, whatever you have available and then carry it back to your central spot (your computer or the corner of your desk, etc...)

2. Take time to prioritize your list. Without assigning value to each task, you will tackle whatever hits you first or whatever you like to do most.

3. Check your list at the end of each day. The purpose of looking over your list is to reassign priorities for the next day.

2. My People Will Get with Your People (Keep a calendar)

Early in my days of being a student pastor I was constantly thinking to myself, "What am I forgetting to do?" So enamored by change I found it hard to keep up with the things that were constant. The only thing I could do was to begin calendaring every event, meeting, service, and Bible study I needed to attend. Keeping a calendar can be the most freeing thing you learn to do. It frees you from the constant worry of "what am I forgetting to do?" and allows you the ability to focus on the task at hand. Consider these things when it comes to organizing your calendar:

1. Put down your givens. Sunday and Wednesday activities and work from there.
2. Put a beginning and ending time to meetings.
3. Use different colors to emphasize priority.
4. Once a week look 6 months out.
5. Keep only one calendar.
6. Give your spouse the first look and first priority when scheduling.
7. Look at your calendar every day.

3. No More Wing and a Prayer Services (Plan your Bible studies in advance)

We have all been guilty of asking God to give us a home run hit while walking up to the plate. Maybe you were caught with a speaking engagement by surprise. Perhaps you had been sick. But valid excuses are very few and very far between. Talking for most of us is not hard. So the thought of figuring out what we are going to say in advance almost seems like a waste of time, right?! We couldn't be more wrong. This is one of the biggest contributing areas to the lack of respect for student pastors. More often than not, we spend hours figuring out the music and planning activities and minutes preparing the Bible study. I came to a realization about four years ago when a student approached me after a Wednesday night youth meeting. I asked him if he liked the program and what he enjoyed most. The kid went on for ten minutes and didn't once mention anything about the Bible study or anything remotely spiritual. God used that young man to get my attention. I had become great at entertaining but lost my focus of shepherding. Jesus' words to Peter rang clear in my head, "If you love me you will feed my sheep." (John 21:17) By being prepared . . .

- You are less likely to repeat yourself.
- You will say more in fewer words when you have practiced and thought your sermon or devotional through.
- You are less likely to lose track or chase rabbits.
- You speak clearer and are clearly understood.
- You are less likely to ramble or repeat yourself. (Just kidding!)

For a deeper look into preparing Bible studies check out chapter 5, To Prepare Bible Studies.

4. Under "C" for Christmas! (Make folders and notebooks for each event, series, and program)

The benefit of keeping notebooks and files for events and programs is primarily to find information. Notebooks help you keep all your facts about a program or event in one central spot. When putting a notebook together make sure to include the following:

For Events
1. Contact names
2. Dates, times, places, and costs
3. Any correspondence to you or from you (Letters, postcards, emails, etc...)
4. Maps and timelines
5. Copies of promotional pieces
6. The Bible studies and handouts

For Programs
1. Study notes
2. Schedule of days on and days off
3. Handouts
4. Leader notes
5. People resources (phone numbers, addresses, etc...)
6. Copies of promotional pieces

You also want to make sure and label your notebook so it is easily distinguished.

5. Bueller? Bueller? (Keep attendance records)

There is much debate about the importance of keeping track of numbers, but the fact is, numbers help tell the story. Low numbers don't make you a bad student pastor as much as big numbers don't make you a good student pastor. There are all sorts of variables that influence your students' attendance. But keeping up with their attendance will help you know valuable information that will help you be a great student pastor. Things like:
- What series or Bible studies seem to peak their interest.
- What times of the year you will have greater numbers of students in attendance.
- What times of the year you will have the most visitors.
- Which programs are meeting the needs of certain groups of students.
- What events are still working.

I keep attendance records for each program we have. Then I make a monthly and semi-annual report that tracks attendance. We have totally renovated and overhauled some of our programs and events because of the track record of attendance. Did a low attendance mean I was a bad student pastor? No. But if I had ignored the numbers I would be. Keeping up with numbers helps you know where you need to improve and where you are being efficient and effective.

6. The Three "Ables" (Set identifiable, quantifiable, and attainable goals)

For most of us, our problem is not that we lack ability or vision. We merely lack the discipline of setting goals to see our vision become reality. Goal setting can be a great help or hindrance. Setting goals will bring you success in your ministry or cause you to continually feel like a failure.

The difference is found in **how** you set goals. "To be a growing youth group" is not a very good goal. But neither is "to have 500 students on Wednesday night" if you normally have 20. Set a goal that has a numerical or visualized end.

A very good friend and fellow pastor was once challenging me in a particular area of my ministry. I came back to him with some goals that I thought would revolutionize my ministry at the time. With an equal amount of grace and candor he looked over my lofty list of goals and replied, "Only set goals on factors you can control" and then handed the list back to me. In my anxiousness to defend myself I quickly grabbed the list and stammered for a reply. But he was right. Almost every goal I had set for the next year was based on factors on which I had no control. I couldn't control how many students came on a Wednesday or a Sunday. I couldn't control how many students trusted Jesus in a year or how many were baptized. I immediately sat down and started a new list. I realized my goals needed to be set according to factors I had control over. Instead of giving a number to how many students accepted Jesus, I set a number on how many times I would share Jesus with someone. After that experience I came up with the more simplified and much shorter list that follows:

1. To share Jesus 100 times in the next year.
2. To eat at school lunches three times a week.
3. To pray daily for every one of my students.
4. To write every student a note once a month.

That was it. And it worked. All the lofty goals I intended to set for Wednesday attendance and baptisms were surpassed by the actual numbers at the end of that year.

Good goals follow four criteria:

1. You have the power to control their variables.
2. They can be measured.
3. They stretch you from where you are to where you need to be.
4. They are actually attainable.

For instance, I have a vision of reaching every student in my city for Christ in a positive way. That does not mean that every student will come to our church or youth group. It simply means, each student in our town will hear about Jesus, His love, and be encouraged by His love through some facet of our ministry. That's my vision. After accepting that as a vision I set out to form goals to help me realize that vision. Speaking 20 times a year in schools, visiting three school lunches a week, attending 2 sporting events a week, and spending two Monday nights a month doing home visits are goals that will help me accomplish that vision.

To further help illustrate my point I have a bad list and a good list of goals.

Bad Goals List
1. Have 75 at a Wednesday night program.
2. 30 students trust Jesus as Lord and Savior.
3. Have the largest youth group in town.
4. Lead 10 students to commit to full time ministry.

Maybe these are all things you would like or maybe even would cast as a vision to your leadership. But as far as goals go, these are no good. Either you feel like a failure because you don't achieve those numbers or you base your success on faulty evidence.

Good Goals List
1. Be prepared for Bible study 2 days in advance.
2. Read 1 book a week.
3. Read the Bible through in a year.
4. Share Jesus 25 times.
5. Pray daily for students.
6. Take a leadership adult to lunch once a week.
7. Invest in leadership students once a month.
8. Train a student to take over Powerpoint or the sound board.

One final thought concerning setting goals would be that you must have a method for holding yourself accountable. Whether you use accountability partners or give your list of goals to your pastor, accountability is key. Without it, you are simply writing down dreams. And often times our dreams are merely hopes that never become realities.

7. August to July (Plan a year at a time)

Scheduling ministry is like putting together a big puzzle. There are certain edge pieces I need to begin with to make sure everything else fits inside. Not that you ever want to plan God out of anything, but at least give some forethought. Sit down and look at your calendar for a year at a time. Brainstorm different topics that would be good to cover at certain times of the year. Know which events are your edge pieces and go from there.

What are our givens? Christmas, Easter, Spring Break, Summer Camp, Mission Trips, Valentine's Day, etc... Begin there and fill in pieces around it. This planning is for events, Bible studies, youth retreats, camps, outreach events, and everything else you find your students being involved in. Planning in advance gives you 4 definite advantages:

1. It will save you money. Most places give early bird specials for early registration.
2. You are guaranteed a spot at camps and events.
3. You can give parents a good idea of the total cost of events for the year.
4. It will save you time.

You also may want to consider putting certain spiritual emphasis at particular times of the year. For example, around Valentine's, Bible studies on abstinence, love, and dating are appropriate. At the beginning of school in August is a good time to push spiritual disciplines because that is a good start-up time. You could also hit spiritual disciplines again in January. In our ministry, March is when lots of students begin to get busy with baseball, softball, and more so we try to do a huge series on commitment to God around that time. April or May is a great time to address dress and encourage your young ladies and men to reserve their bodies for their mate. If you wait until June, they have already bought their swimsuits. Talk about it early enough that they will be thinking about what you said while they are trying them on. These are just a few thoughts. Knowing your students and the battles they face will help you in this process. Looking at your calendar a year at a time will cause the parents to think you are intentional and purposeful with their students.

Blueprint #5

To Prepare Bible Studies

To Prepare Bible Studies
1. "Feed My Sheep" (Always teach the Bible)
2. Like a Beautiful Song (Make notes, no matter how simple, and follow them)
3. Like a Parable (Use illustrations from life that students can relate to)
4. Life is Like a Cantaloupe! (Use visual aids)
5. Stand Up, Sit Down, Turn Around! (Worship flow is critical)
6. Nacho Mamma's Restaurant (Use the series approach)
7. Put the Rock Over Here! (Build set designs)
8. B-L-A-N-K-O (Use handouts to teach)
9. The Picasso Plan (Develop a one year strategy of lessons)

1. "Feed My Sheep" (Always teach the Bible)

No matter how eloquent you believe your delivery to be or how powerful your illustrations are . . . God's Word is what changes lives. One of my gravest frustrations is when a speaker spends 30 minutes telling you about how bad he was before he was a Christian and then takes two minutes to tell you how much Jesus loves you and how to have a relationship with Him. I am all for waxing your speaking ability and keeping your delivery fresh. I think mixing things up and using fun, creative, and sometimes off-the-wall illustrations and objects are great . . . but preach Jesus! Three times Jesus reiterated the importance and necessity of feeding His sheep. (John 21:17)

The following are some questions you can answer as you are laying out your outline to make sure Christ is at the center of your Bible study, testimony, or sermon.

1. Who do I mention more, God or myself?
2. When people leave, what will they most remember?
3. Will the stories I tell make a direct connection to a spiritual thought in their minds?

2. Like a Beautiful Song (Make notes, no matter how simple, and follow them)

This one little tip can dramatically change your delivery and your effectiveness. Making notes will keep you from chasing rabbits, help you focus on your main point, and give your hearers a sense of understanding. I know that there are times when each of us has been called on at the last minute to give a short Bible study or lesson. These times are few and far between. More often than that, we simply just do not give appropriate planning time to our studies. The more you study and know exactly what you want to say and how you want to say it, the clearer your own notes will be to you.

Sermon or Bible study notes can be a 1, 2, 3 outline, a word-for-word script, or anything in between. I prefer having memorized my main points, illustrations, and references. I have found that when I do that, God brings to life the ability of my spiritual gift of preaching and teaching. The following is a list of what I include in my notes.

1. Sermon title and date
2. Scriptures (main passage, if relatively short, written out)
3. Supporting Scriptures
4. Main points

5. Illustrations
6. Discussion questions
7. What actions I want them to take as a result of hearing the lesson

3. Like a Parable (Use illustrations from life that students can relate to)

Adding a story about life that your students can relate to will add a dimension of reality to your Bible studies. It gives a physiological peg for them to hang an idea or concept on. And that is what you want, because grasping knowledge and gaining understanding is part of growing spiritually. Paul wrote it in Philippians 1:9-11 this way, "And this is my prayer: that your love may abound more and more in knowledge and depth of insight, so that you may be able to discern what is best and may be pure and blameless until the day of Christ, filled with the fruit of righteousness that comes through Jesus Christ – to the glory and praise of God." You share God's true Word in a real way that they can comprehend and they begin to change from the inside out.

The other danger is that you become over loaded on the illustration side and light on the Bible side. Make direct connections between story parts and scripture. The only fear is that you get a great illustration but it doesn't match your point. It is just a great illustration. Take time to study and match your illustrations with your scriptures. The process should be:

1. Spend daily time with God.
2. Out of that daily time, God speaks to you about direction for Bible studies.
3. Study it through in your personal walk with God.
4. Decipher what are the main points you feel led to get across from scripture.
5. Then, look for your illustrations.
6. Practice giving your illustrations.

A good practice would be to catalog your illustrations. You can buy lots of books with wonderful ideas in them. When you use an illustration out of a book, put the date and the event somewhere on that page. If you have illustrations you think up or have heard, write them down. Writing them down will help you know them better, too. Then keep a file for illustrations.

A bad illustration is like telling a joke that has no punch line . . . it just goes on and on and on and then finally stops sometime after everyone has quit paying attention.

4. Life is Like a Cantaloupe! (Use visual aids)

Every student likes object lessons. Students will remember a sermon or Bible study longer when there is an object that they can identify the message with. There is something about us, we are visual people. Using an object in your message will bring to life a concept and cause your student to think about that concept days and sometimes months later. Vacuum cleaners, clocks, blow torches (use with caution), dozers, cement, and more, used correctly, will jog your students' minds to remember your Bible study. Here are a few guidelines to using objects:

1. Wait to show it until you want to make the point with the object. It adds suspense and keeps them from being distracted.
2. Make sure it works. Whether it is a simple magic trick or an electrical hand tool, make sure you have tried it out before hand.
3. Be safe with objects. Carelessness will not set well with parents and students may try some of the things you do.
4. Make sure the object has a direct and obvious connection to your point. You don't want them to have to make a huge stretch to get it. The easier it is to get the connection, the more likely they are to think of your point when they see the object the next time.

5. Stand Up, Sit Down, Turn Around! (Worship flow is critical)

You do not want to condition students like rats in a cage. But you do want to create a distraction free environment where the Holy Spirit can work easily on the hearts of your students. Therefore, make sure and create a flow chart for your service that allows the fun, the serious, and everything in between. Here are some hints to designing a smooth flow for a worship service:

1. Begin with prayer. It is almost like calling the meeting to order. Even if you are getting ready to blow the roof off with loud music, begin with an upbeat, earnest prayer of thanks.
2. Learn how to use fast, transitional, and slow music. This isn't complicated.
    a. Make a list of all the music you sing.
    b. Put them in three categories; fast, medium, and slow.
    c. Go through and pull songs from each category to make a 3, 5, or 6 song play list.

**Quick Note: Use a live praise band of your students. Even if it is just one kid, it will begin to allow them to see themselves as participators and not just spectators. Once we started using a live praise band of our own students we saw a huge spiritual spike in the music part of our services as a whole.*

3. Know there truly is a three minute rule in effect. Students need a laugh, surprise, or illustration every three minutes to help keep their attention. Adults can handle a little bit longer, but not much.
4. Change up the flow sometimes and experiment. I have found that middle school students in our ministry tend to need all the music at one time and then the entire Bible study at one time. High schoolers on the other hand can handle mixing up the pot a little bit. The regimented diet helps assimilate the middle schoolers better.
5. There must be a point of action. No matter if it is a three minute testimony, or a 30 minute sermon, you are speaking to inspire, encourage, and to motivate them to action. Know what it is you want them to do. Write it down in your notes. Share it before you begin, in the middle of your lesson, and reiterate it clearly at the end.

Worship flow can either be one of your greatest allies or one of your biggest worries. Remember, flexibility is the key. You should be equipping students to do much of your ministry. And any time you are giving students the opportunity to step up . . . there will be mistakes. Work through them graciously and know that if they did everything perfectly, there would not be a need for your position.

6. Nacho Mamma's Restaurant (Use the series approach)

I have grown such a passion and conviction about this one area that it almost merits its own chapter or book. The series approach to Bible studies really does work.

We generally have three to five series studies a semester. The series identity is simply a way to package what God has laid on our heart to share. When you package your Bibles studies in a series, it causes you to approach Bible study intentionally and procedurally. For instance, one of my friends had heard some silly advertisement for a fake restaurant called "Nacho Mamma's". I had felt led to work on a series that would teach and encourage students to have their own faith. A Bible study series that detailed the personal relationship of Christianity and the personal discipleship that comes with it. We decorated our stage to look like a Mexican restaurant and made up cool shirts for the four week series. We even wrote skits for each week that helped point to our focus for the night. The catch phrase was, "It's YOUR faith . . . Nacho Mamma's!"

As useful as series have been here are some guidelines we have come to accept:
1. Keep all series between 3 and 6 weeks. Longer than that and students lose focus.
2. Use set and stage designs. See number 7 of this chapter.
3. Take breaks between series to do stand-alone Bible studies.
4. Use handouts but not all the time and make sure they aren't predictable but logical.
5. Change up your presentation flow and technology.

Where do you get series ideas? For a creative mind that is looking for where God is working, you can find ideas all around you. Five really good places to look for series ideas are:
1. Movies
2. Walks of life (cowboys, sports, etc...)
3. Fads (clothes)

4. Food and restaurants
5. Other books

The Momentum of Interest Theory

Why are March Madness, the World Series, and the Super Bowl such great successes? Because they are all able to maintain a certain level of unequivocal momentum. So what is this momentum that allows each of these events to keep people motivated to watch, participate, and cheer year after year? It is the momentum of interest! They are able to keep it fresh, exciting, and seemingly new - interesting! But not by changing the game. By changing how they **package** the game. Everything from halftime — half-court shots for a million dollars to the drama of inside stories on players; we are railed along on the train of intrigue until we buy, watch, and emulate the game. If we could, would, only do the same with the greatest and most important message your students will ever know. I believe we don't have the attention of our students for four basic reasons. We are . . .

A. Out of tune. We are not scratching where they are itching.
B. Out of touch. We are boring.
C. Out of character. We are not living what we are teaching.
D. Out of step. We are so unorganized that we are distracting from our message.

Sure, our three points and witty object lesson may have worked on a group of students back when we were in youth group but we also didn't have X Box, DVDs, or internet. We have to keep the message the same but change up the package.

7. Put the Rock Over Here! (Build set designs)

The idea of anything you do with your stage design is to enhance the Bible study. You could create a real ghost town on your stage or in your youth area, but if it doesn't act as a tool to help you better present God's Word, it is shallow and at best, cool to look at.

Here is a process for thinking through a set or stage design.

1. **What is the theme of the series?** Not just golf or fast food but what are the spiritual aspects I want to communicate first and foremost?

2. **What objects or surroundings communicate that series?** If I am doing a baseball series called "Take Me Out to The Ball Game" that is all about relating aspects of baseball to the Christian life, how would I decorate? Make the middle of my stage look like home plate with chain link fence behind me and a life size cut out of an umpire. Throw some pennants up on the walls, set out some balls and gloves and a scoreboard. Make up Bible study notes that look like programs and there you have the beginnings of a set design your students will remember. And if they remember it, they can apply it.

3. **What space do I have to work with?** If you have a 12'X12' room, you can't do the big chain link thing, but you could do a much smaller version.

4. **What pieces of stage decor do I need to fill the space to communicate the series?** Exactly what props or pieces will I need to make the Bible study points come alive?

(For a series we did called "Army of the ONE", I went to the local Army Surplus store and spent around $250. I bought old parachutes, army tents, back packs, shell casings, camo netting, and more and then transformed our stage to look like a base camp. We put a small fan in one of the parachutes to create movement and panned a yellow light across the front of it. And just a little bit of smoke from a fog machine will go a long way. But then for a series we did called Most eXtreme Elimination Challenge of your Faith" we simply put black tarp on the stage and cleared everything else off.)

8. B-L-A-N-K-O (Use handouts to teach)

As student pastors we really need to know the difference between preaching and teaching. Preaching is a word, given to you by God, to convict, encourage, uplift, and to inspire your students to action. Teaching is the discipling part of our ministry when we help students grow their own faith. It is during teaching moments that I most like to use handouts. Handouts help me to correctly state Biblical information, to stay on track and to keep all the students engaged. Handouts also help the students stay focused and gives them a point of reference if they want to use the information later. (I don't even pretend to think that the students keep all these handouts for a long period of time. But they will keep them for a little while. And every time they read it, they are going back over that truth.)

Handout Helps:
- Do not use them all the time.
- Stay away from the two B's; boring and busy. Try using some color and work to keep it easy to read. If it is so full and busy that they can't find a place to write down notes, they won't.
- Make enough for everyone.

So now that we are sold on the idea of using handouts for teaching, what's next? We have to know the best time to use them and the best way to use them. Black ink on white paper is just not creative enough in our world where students are bombarded with HD TV and super color images on XBox and Play Station. We are passing along truth that is supremely more important than all the world has to offer. So do your best to follow these four guidelines when making handouts.

1. Reserve blanks for key words.
2. Avoid the two B's; package it in a way that is appealing to the students.
3. Use same format for a series.
4. Give them space to make notes.

Always push your purpose. On every piece of printed material we put out, we paste on our logo and most often our purpose statement. We will change the font, the size, and the placement, but like Ragu, it's in there.

How often should you use handouts?

I know the idea of using handouts seems so rudimentary, but there is actually a little more to a successful handout. The bottom line is that the students read it and take it with them. Once a week may be too predictable while once a quarter may leave them wondering what they are supposed to do with the paper with blanks on it.

9. The Picasso Plan (Develop a one year strategy of lessons)

One of the greatest ways I can honor God as a student pastor is by being prepared. That transcends the memorization of points, stories, and music. Being truly prepared starts way back in the planning process. Developing a year long plan will enhance your Bible studies and take a huge amount of undue strain off your ministry. Many times we approach our ministries like it is a kid's coloring book and we only have four crayons. Planning helps make all the things you *do* look more like a Picasso than an etch-a-sketch drawing. Our ministries should be marked with not only intensity and passion, but also creativity and a certain amount of mystery. When you plan months out, you are allowing yourself the room to create a Picasso rather than a "paint by numbers" picture of Mary with her little lamb.

A big picture plan doesn't have to have all the details. It is going through and putting up the big strokes of paint on your canvas. We never want to plan God out of something but you can prayerfully lay out the skeleton of your year.

When doing this I usually find a time when I can invest several hours of uninterrupted thought. I begin by answering some key questions.
1. What issues are students facing that I need to address?
2. What events, programs, and holidays do I need to plan around? (Beginning of school, Prom, Christmas, etc...)
3. What Bible knowledge do I want them to grasp?
4. What days do I have to work with? Go over your calendar to see how Sundays and Wednesdays (or whatever days you meet) fall. If you have 4 Wednesdays between a holiday and a special service, that would be a great place to put a 4 week series.

The priorities are as follows:
- What needs to be said (the message)
- When to say it (the schedule)
- How to say it (the package)

An essential part of planning is to find where the gaps are. Find in what areas your students are struggling and where they need to grow spiritually. Over the past five years our ministry has established some foundational principles that we want every student to know and understand before they graduate and leave us. We use those foundational principles to steer our planning process. Joining peak interest times of the year with those principles gives us a big picture plan. For instance, we know that at the beginning of a school year and the beginning of a new year are great times to push spiritual disciplines. It is a time when they are thinking of getting started off on the right foot or a time when they are thinking about making changes for the better.

You don't have to set these plans in stone and live hard and fast by them. But without a plan you will wander from one Wednesday night to the next with no continuity or direction. Whether you take two days each semester to get away in a hotel room or lock yourself in your house and turn off the phone, planning the big picture is more than necessary . . . it is imperative to be effective.

Blueprint # 6

To Assimilate Parents and Workers

Part One

1. Wait Until You See the Whites of Their Eyes! (Make lunch dates, not phone calls)
2. Don't Make Them Guess! (Communicate regularly and clearly)

Part Two

3. Somebody HELP! (Getting committed couples to minister along side you)
4. The Team Approach (Build a ministry team of parents)
5. Easy as 1-2-3! (Make it easy for parents to help with big projects)
6. Called and Equipped (Have worker training events)
7. You Are More Than Kind! (Show respect and thanks for your leaders)
8. We Want YOU! (Recruiting parents and adults)

When it comes to explaining parent and adult involvement and their impact on your ministry, a really vivid mental picture comes to mind . . . my first s'more. I was just a kid and our Sunday School teacher took us for a camp out. Six boys standing side by side around a small fire with wire clothes hangers stretched toward the orange glow. Each metal spear holding so many marshmallows that the hangers began to sag down toward the flames. The instructions sounded simple enough, "Brown your marshmallow to the desired color, pull it off the hanger, and slap it between two graham crackers with some chocolate." But what followed proved to be nothing short of a small disaster. As my mound of mallows dipped deep into the flames, they didn't slowly turn to a desired brown . . . they caught fire. Then in a whipping motion to retrieve my flame licked treat back, part of the mallow (on fire mind you) hurled passed me and rested with an audible "splat" on my Sunday School teacher's arm. He was screaming, I was screaming, we were all screaming. He finally blew it out and covered his arm with a damp cloth. But the fun didn't end there. From there the plan was to remove the once flaming and certainly burnt mallow from the hanger and place it onto the graham cracker. My fingers sank through the mallow as I tried to gently but not successfully pull it off. Finally, with a lot of fumbling, I slid some mass of mallow, I don't know if it was one or three, and put it between the graham cracker. While reaching for the other piece and the chocolate, my fingers, clad with stickiness, left a small but lasting trail on the box, the makeshift table, and everything else I came close to. But I was not the only one experiencing this. The rest of my buddies had much the same results. For a group of 4th graders it wasn't too bad but certainly complicated by anyone's standards. And that is parent involvement in student ministry; complicated by anyone's standards, but just as sweet as that S'MORE was. So is the peace and joy of having parents and adults investing in your ministry.

As I grew older and wiser I began to learn there are ways of not getting the mallow all over the place. I learned the skillful art of browning a marshmallow and now consider myself a useful camper with mallow tanning ability. Each year as our youth group enjoys a canoe trip, one of my favorite activities is making s'mores. While many students are wiping and licking their fingers, trying to transfer their melted mallow to the graham cracker, I have with the meticulousness of a master chef finished my s'more. And the treat is, in the words of Tony the Tiger, GGGRRRREEEEAAATTTT!

Parent and adult involvement in youth ministry can be so sticky and complicated that many student pastors try to remove parents all together. They either try to fly solo or recruit college students to pump up their ministry. Sometimes a younger student pastor sees the parents as a threat because they feel like a kid around them. Other times student pastors wear themselves ragged because they are afraid to ask for help. They adopt the "It's my job to do it" mentality. A pastor's job is to equip the saints and not to do all the work himself. (Ephesians 4:12) Other student pastors, reaching for the independence of doing their *own* thing their *own* way, will employ a crew of college students who will **do** without asking questions. I don't think using interns is a bad thing but there is nothing that can replace the heart and life of active parents investing in your ministry. Without their involvement you have not only alienated a rich resource of people but you have doomed yourself.

Once upon a time my strategy was to plan and do everything myself. It seemed like a good plan at the time, but I didn't like what it yielded. Parents, instead of being champions of my ministry encouraging their kids to attend, were spending most of their time in conversation with me questioning what was going on. Not in an accusatory way but in a "Hey, we feel out of the loop" way. Finally my pea brain grasped the concept. Involve more parents and I will in essence involve more students. Involve more parents and I get to spend more time doing the things in ministry I like to do. Involve more parents and (Wow) other parents want to come be a part, too.

For all general purposes this chapter is divided into two basic parts. The first part has to do with assimilating parents who are not really involved. These are parents who need to be communicated to but aren't leading in any particular way. The second part is all about assimilating your parent and adult workers. (I say parent and adult because not all of your workers may be parents.) Grasp and employ the concepts of this chapter and your ministry will grow. Your time with your family will increase. Your joy will blossom.

Part One

1. Wait Until You See the Whites of Their Eyes! (Make lunch dates, not phone calls)

In a day and age where nearly every parent and student alike has a cell phone, many times our answer to communication barriers is to give a quick ring. But when it comes to initiating meaningful dialogue with a parent, face-to-face is a must. Whether it is to discuss the special need of their student or to ask them to take a responsibility in your ministry, make a lunch or supper meeting with them. Especially when it comes to tough or sensitive issues, there is body language that cannot be suggested via the air waves of a phone. If you are like me, most of the time when I am on the phone I am easily distracted by the things going on around me. That distraction can be perceived as an air of not caring from the other end of the phone line.

If checking to make sure Mrs. Johnson is bringing cookies Sunday, a phone call is fine. But something about her child or even asking her to lead a small group deserves an eyeball to eyeball meeting. The following are some hints to help you in this process.

1. Always set a beginning and ending time.
2. Be prepared to talk and have all your information together. People will only follow people who are leading.
3. Offer and then be prepared to pay for meals.
4. Choose places to meet that will help you. If talking to a parent about a very serious matter involving their student don't take them to lunch at one of the more busy places in town. Meet in their home or your office. If asking someone to consider being the team leader for a big event, take them to lunch at a place with lots of energy and bright, cheerful waiters and waitresses.

2. Don't Make Them Guess! (Communicate regularly and clearly)

Utilizing and involving parents will be much like stretching a chain between two vehicles. You will be only as strong as your weakest link. So what keeps the links strong? Communication! There are two criteria when it comes to communication. You must communicate regularly and you must communicate clearly. They are both equally important. You must treat them like twin toddlers in the cleaner aisle (those of you who have kids will actually visualize this); they need constant attention!

In answering three simple questions you can know where to begin.

What Do I Communicate?

You can make hints and reminders of your passion and purpose for your ministry in written communication but the heart of your passion and purpose must be expressed through you directly. Make sure that you verbalize face-to-face and sell your ministry to your adults. They need to hear from your own mouth the passion you have for ministry and the love you have for their students. You cannot replace the physiological and emotional advantage of facial expression and voice fluctuation as you sincerely bare your heart to parents. No letter could ever accomplish what you could in person.

So what do I put in writing? "Only the facts, ma'am!" Use written communication to reiterate your passion but primarily to communicate dates, times, places, and cost. Before I print any postcard, flyer, poster or letter I look to make sure that I have answered the "Big Four" - who, what, where, and when.

Who is this event, Bible study, or trip for? What is this event, Bible study, or trip and what does it cost? Where is this thing going to be? When are we leaving and getting back (dates and times)?

*Try to put your youth group logo on every piece of printed material you put out. Just like branding companies do for major corporations, you are creating another level of awareness and consciousness for your ministry in the minds of your students and adults.

How Do I Communicate?

You can employ a whole gamut of communications pieces. The trick is to find what works for you and your people. The following is a list of communication options.

- Parent meetings (big group style)
- Parent conferences (private, in your office)
- Monthly newsletter
- Bulletin announcements
- Email
- Flyers

- Personal letters
- Personal phone calls
- Phone trees
- Student hand-outs (they take home with them)
- Parent news board (in a hallway or in your youth room)

When Do I Communicate?

Regularly! By establishing a regular forum for communicating to parents you do away with "fly by the seat of your pants" ministry and enable yourself the benefit of time; time to work things out and be prepared. For us, the following scenario works.

Newsletter – this gives the parents all the dates, times, locations, etc… in a package they can easily read and save. A good rule of thumb is to generate a parent newsletter as often as you create a student newsletter. Monthly during the school year and one for the summer works well.

Parent Meetings – get parents together twice a year to discuss schedules, summer trips, and major issues.

Parent Conferences – offer one night meetings or Saturday seminars on relevant issues facing parents: talking to kids about sex, money management, setting dating parameters, disciplining strong-willed children, etc… Offer these as you recognize the need.

Part Two

3. Somebody HELP! (Getting committed couples to minister along side you)

In all my years of ministry, one of the smartest things I have done was recruiting two couples to come along side me in ministry, and it wasn't even my idea. After spending three years having interns my ministry was getting ready to receive what I thought was a fatal blow. I was losing them.

But in essence it was a true gift from God. One Monday morning I sat in my office with my head in my hands wondering how everything was going to get done. How could I be everywhere? How could I do everything? I believe in delegation but there still has to be someone who knows what is going on. What am I going to do? God really began to wrench my heart and tell me He was in control and not me. So I laid it at His feet and began to pray for His *wisdom* instead of *extra hands*. A few weeks later during a staff meeting one of the other staff members talked about getting a lady in her ministry to help her. Someone who would answer questions the same way she would. I knew right then what to do. Recruit two couples who would come along side Christy and me, who would grow in Christ and do ministry with us. Parents who shared our conviction about ministry and morals and who loved students the way we did.

I began to ask God on a daily basis to bring us the right couples. Maybe they wouldn't be just like us. Let's hope not, I would think. And so He did. Within a few weeks God had solidified in our hearts whom the two couples would be. We set up supper and lunch dates with the couples to share with them our heart and our idea. Before long both couples excitedly agreed.

The idea is to have other people who share your conviction and heart. People who will answer the same way you would but also people who will be strong where you are weak. This is more than just having leaders. This is asking a lay couple to join you in ministry. This, this is commitment.

1. We sought out couples who had younger students. This would mean they would naturally be in our ministry for at least five years.
2. After seeking God's face, we chose two couples who had different leadership styles.
3. We not only do church things together, we do social things together.
4. We let people know they are part of our ministry team.
5. We give them responsibility for projects. (Small group director, ministry team leader, special events coordinator, etc...)

4. The Team Approach (Build a ministry team of parents)

After establishing ministry partners, the second best thing to have is a team of parents who will make up a parent ministry team. These people are not a governing body but rather a sounding board. They are the people who will be your biggest cheerleaders and will help explain your crazy ideas to the other parents. They will be able to use their own words to convey your heart to parents who you may not be able to connect with. There are four major benefits to setting up a ministry team.

1. **Parent representation**. By having a team made up of your parents, you automatically guard your plans and ideas from being challenged by schedules and parental misconceptions. There have been times I have had great ideas but when it came to playing them out in everyday life, they stunk. That ministry team helped me step through the pros and cons and come to a resolution that worked for most students.

2. **Parent involvement**. The natural process of teaming together and sharing your ministry plans, goals, and needs will be for more adults to step up and take responsibility. You will find that they want to help and will come up with more ideas.

3. **Parent awareness**. A weak link in the chain of ministry has always been communication. By employing a team of parents to be your eyes and ears, they will become your mouthpiece as well. They will share your heart to people you never get to talk to. They will help explain your ideas and plans to parents so you can focus on explaining it to students.

4. **Parent support**. There is an intrinsic value to having other people in on the ground floor of your decision making. They have a vested interest.

5. Easy as 1-2-3! (Make it easy for parents to help with big projects)

Many times it is not that parents don't want to help, they are simply intimidated. A fear of not knowing what to do or how to respond lurks heavily in their mind. The fear of being rejected by students weighs in and causes them to quietly stand by. What you must do is make it easy and fun for your adults to be involved. Try the following three concepts when giving adults a job or ministry:

1. Give them a budget. Pretty plain and simple. If you say they have $300 to work with, ask them to turn in receipts for the $300. Let them know that if they want to add to that or get a donation, that is fine, but you are only committing to $300. On much bigger projects it will help to give them an itemized budget. For instance, if a parent is planning your spring retreat, they probably need to know that you have budgeted X number of dollars for a speaker, X for food, X for games, and so on.

2. Give them a general plan and the parameters. You should give them a map or blueprint. This is part of making it simple. Depending on your leader, you may give them points 1 – 2 – 3 or you may have to give them points 1 – 2 – 3 and all the sub-points, too. Sometimes the less you give them, the better. It allows them to use their fresh eyes to pull the project together.

3. Give them an idea of your expectation. After you have shared with them how much they can spend and the plan (however simple or detailed), you set them up to win by giving them reasonable expectations. We do not want to disregard the aspect of faith that is necessary to make any event or project successful in God's eyes, but we do want to set our people up to win. So many times we are guilty of passing the buck and shrugging our shoulders as our people fail and then become disappointed and discouraged. Part of equipping is teaching them how to be successful at leading. Make sure your expectations are reasonable and reachable. If you only have 25 students in your youth group, expecting an adult to plan an event for 150 students is asking for a big let down. Remember, reasonable and reachable.

Once you have given a project or event over to your parents, you must let it go. You still have to maintain accountability but let them do the work. If you step in along the way and give leadership, you are usurping their authority and taking their job away. This will only serve to leave you alone in ministry. If you must criticize or simply ask for something to be changed, do it in love with much grace and only to the person in charge. Outside of moral degradation there are not many valid reasons for you to step in. Be an overseer and let them be the project manager. Very rarely will it look the same as if you had done it but that's okay. This is part of "equipping the saints".

Another aspect is that of parents and adults who help in non-Bible study type functions. Parents can work a snack bar, greet students at the door, or even run sound and lights. Every time you give an adult or parent a responsibility, make sure you are clear in your directions and clear with your expectations. Hint: putting parents and adults on a rotating schedule will keep them from experiencing burn out.

6. Called and Equipped (Have worker training events)

To go along with setting your people up to win is the principle of training leaders. This is a spiritual principle for God always equips those He calls. For us to recruit adults and ask them to do something we have not trained them to do is not good leadership on our part. Training your Bible study leaders and facilitators is essential to the growth or your students and the joy of your leaders. Whether you initiate a continuing education system for your leaders or have a once a year training event, the principle is the same: feed them so they can feed others.

In worker training events, try to cover two areas; purpose and programs. The leaders must catch, grasp, and realize their part in the purpose of your youth ministry before they can lead effectively. Take time with your leaders to cast and recast the vision of your student ministry. They, before anyone else, must be on board. You can tell if you have sufficiently cast the vision by their level of excitement and their commitment to the students. The programs part of training is a basic fundamentals approach to walking them through the steps of leading whatever Bible study they are responsible for. Pass out materials, study sheets, notes, and whatever else they will need to do their ministry. Then cover the mechanics of the study. Cover everything from helping them to consider the time to how to transition from an ice breaker to prayer. Demonstrate for them how to teach, facilitate, and even involve students.

There is also the benefit of building accountability. Without accountability, many leaders will roam off to teach what they are passionate about rather than what you have prayerfully put together. You need to give them room to lead and be individual in their leadership but also keep them on target and on task. Worker training events help you define clear expectations and draw boundary lines. A good leader will respect the lines and even appreciate them.

Training events accomplish four major goals:
1. They allow you to personally cast vision and purpose.
2. They unify your adult team and create synergy.
3. They give you a forum to equip your leaders with tools and knowledge.
4. They build in accountability.

As a caveat to the accountability thought, we ask all our adult leaders to NOT use tobacco or alcohol in any form, period! The conviction is that your ministry will rise to the level of the leaders you gather on your team. Any leader who is spiritually weak to the point of not seeing tobacco use or social drinking as a bad example doesn't need to be shaping Biblical perspectives of impressionable hearts. Any leader who ignores the relevance of it and sneaks it or hides it, not only will be caught but will most likely not be accountable to teach the material. The bottom line is that you are spiritually accountable to God for how you lead your ministry. Placing people with addictions and habits that are deemed as harmful and wrong in our society is to ignore your responsibility of spiritual leader.

After the training, the next best habit is to start meeting regularly with your leaders. It is not a complicated plan but it works. Meet with your leaders as often as you can without exhausting them. You will very seldom have every worker there because of schedules and extracurricular activities, but try. And when you do meet, meet for a purpose and set a time to begin and finish.

When you come together, make sure you have an agenda or plan. Never, I repeat, never go into a meeting of your leaders without a plan.

Part of that plan should be to make it worth their time. And having a set starting and ending time will help you stay on task during your meeting and keep you from chasing too many rabbits.

Survey your leaders to find out when the best time to meet will be. You can determine that by the time when the largest number of your leaders can attend. Then communicate the meeting time to them. Usually a letter two weeks out, a phone call a week out and a postcard a few days before the meeting is sufficient. Don't expect them to show up if you haven't reminded them. Be a leader for your leaders! Leaders are pro-active more often than they are re-active.

7. You Are More Than Kind! (Show respect and thanks for your leaders)

In high school I had a buddy who was the care free sort of fella, never thinking about the weightier things of life. He burned the engine up in his truck. I mean, that joker, his engine, stopped and wouldn't go anymore. Upon closer investigation by his father and a mechanic they pinpointed my friend's problem. He had run the truck, apparently for weeks, without any oil in it. I am no mechanic and don't understand exactly how or why it broke the engine, but I can tell you this. As a 17 year old, I regularly checked the oil in my car.

Much like oil in an engine, you must constantly be working behind the scenes when it comes to your leaders. Your leaders need two kinds of oil: respect and appreciation. Anyone working for weeks and months on end, without appreciation will finally get to the point where they say enough is enough. It only takes one time of you ignoring or not respecting them in front of students before you lose them. The following is a list of things you can do to respect and appreciate your parents and adult leaders.

Ways To Show Your Love and Respect

1. Appreciation Dinner – Something where your leaders don't have to do a thing. Maybe it is catered or even put together and presented by your older youth.

2. Always handle problems one-on-one – Do your best to steer clear of ugly scenes in public places.

3. Get Bible study leaders their materials well in advance – They need time to read through and digest what you are asking them to teach.

4. Personal notes after an event – Just a quick note to let them know you appreciate their effort and work.

5. Addressing them properly in front of students – Mr. or Mrs. or whatever is socially acceptable in your area. But always respectful.

6. Publicly thank them – They may not like this at first but it is good for you, necessary for your students, and it will be great for the adults.

7. Give them gift certificates for extra service – Not for everything they do, but there are times when they go above and beyond. Buy them a gift card so they can go out as a couple for a nice dinner or something.

8. Never undermine their authority – Even when you disagree with them, you must do it with tact and love. You must be careful how you react in front of students.

9. Budget to pay their way to events – Many times we ask a lot of our adult leaders financially because we want them to be at every event to build connections with the students but then we forget to consider the financial strain. Budget to help them be there.

10. Take a leader retreat – Plan a time for their families to go relax after a busy year. This is best done when planned for somewhere close and planned well in advance.

11. Service plaques – Somewhere in your youth room, post or hang a plaque that has the names of your workers.

12. Include them in planning – Pull your adult leaders into the planning phase to talk about the specifics of events and Bible studies. This is a great way to show that you appreciate them, by listening and using their ideas.

13. Good ole phone call or email – It is quick and precise.

14. Special pictures – If there is a good picture of one of your leaders with some students, print it on the computer with the name of the event labeled at the bottom and mail it to them with a thank you note.

8. We Want YOU! (Recruiting parents and adults)

So all this sounds great . . . if you have adults and parents willing to work. What happens if you don't have people lined up at your door waiting to be challenged with the next wonderful idea that pops into your head? Recruit! Go get them. No one will care as much about your ministry as you do until you cast the vision and share your passion. Parents can get the fish bowl syndrome; they only see the glass in front of their face and miss the whole room beyond the bowl. So help them by taking your need to them. Here are some ways you can share your leadership needs.

1. Make announcements in church bulletin.
2. Send notes home with students.
3. Put an ad or story about your need in the parent newsletter.
4. Personally call or write parents.

The following is a list, not exhaustive by any means, of ways to involve your parents and adults.

1. Small group teacher/facilitator.
2. Lead a drama team.
3. Run sound and lights.
4. Take care of food and snacks.
5. Open and close the building.
6. Coordinate special events and functions.
7. Patrol the parking lot.
8. Keep the peace during Bible study.

As your ministry grows you will understand more and more not only the spiritual principle involved in "equipping the saints" but also the mere necessity of investing in leaders. For many of us student pastors, it is not the working with students that gets us into trouble. It is the lack of organization, communication, and appreciation of our adults that puts our ministries in jeopardy. There are no Lone Rangers in student ministry. Apply the basic ideas mentioned here that fit your ministry and style and you will begin to see a change in your adults.

Blueprint # 7

To Grow Student Leaders

To Grow Student Leaders
1. R.E.S.P.E.C.T. (Give away little bits of responsibility with accountability)
2. Disciple, More Than Just an Eight Letter Word (Have a set plan for discipling new Christians)
3. It's a Memory Game! (Memorize scripture with them)
4. My House is Your House (Spend time with them in your home)
5. Road Trip 1 (Take them to conferences with you)
6. Road Trip 2 (Take them with you to speaking engagements)
7. Your Turn! (Give them opportunities to speak, lead, or direct)

We all eat. Most of us really enjoy eating, especially McDonald's fries with a chocolate shake, and yes sometimes it is hard for me to focus. Oh yea, growing leaders. My point, we live in a culture where we don't know what it is to have to clean and cook a meal. We can pull up in our cars to a window, yell our order into a metal box and drive up 30 feet to another window and in three minutes pull out 2 Big Macs, fries, and a couple of super sized drinks. No wonder our kids think that cooking at home takes too long. So where am I going with this? Just stick with me.

I ease up to the stop light and can see the traffic going the other direction has a yellow light. Instinctively I begin to push the gas and the break at the same time as I anxiously anticipate the light turning green. I guess that allows me the greatest leverage against the people in the lane next to me to make sure I "win" to the next light. For goodness sake! It's a stop light. Two or three minutes tops! My point is that we are prisoners of fast food and speedy service and have lost our ability to be patient.

Not only have most of us lost the ability to be patient, we have never had it. Patience is a virtue. It builds character and tolerance in you that keeps you from going crazy in an imperfect world. And patience is the first component in growing leaders. Your students may have defining moments where they step up to a challenge and walk off the other side having realized their potential and seen the big picture, but their leadership is still a process of growth. And those two words, "process" and "growth" both equal "time."

The other component of growing leaders is purpose. From the moment you meet some students, you know they have leadership qualities and traits. Others will rise to a position of leadership due to tragedy or necessity or even some freak or unforeseen incident. We can't tell God who should be leaders, but once He shows us or them, we must do our best to train them and take them to the next level. Help them answer "What should I lead?", "How do I lead?", and "What will be my leadership style?" Developing a purposeful plan and helping them answer these questions will be the difference in you having students with leadership potential and you having student leaders.

1. R.E.S.P.E.C.T. (Give away little bits of responsibility with accountability)

Attila the Hun, while not a very good example of how to love Jesus, did offer good examples of developing and maintaining leadership. He led by example in everything he did. He always did first what he asked his men to do. Alexander the Great also exampled leadership in the way he ushered his men into battle. And Christ was tempted in all ways that we are tempted so He could sympathize with us. Great leaders don't just find other leaders, they grow leaders.

The first key is earning and giving respect. As your students and adults see you example a lifestyle of earning and giving respect, they will begin to emulate that behavior. The following are some tips to help you earn and maintain respect.

1. Always let the girls go first. This teaches your young men to be gentlemen and to treat girls with respect.
2. As the leader, you go last. But don't sit down and complain, use that time to walk around and visit with each person there. They will notice you go last even though a word may never be said. That means you are showing them respect.
3. Don't interrupt and don't allow yourself to be interrupted. When you interrupt someone that means you think you are more important than what they are talking about. When you allow yourself to be interrupted, you teach that every little thing is more important than you.
4. Expect people to make appointments. Stay away from drop in visits.
5. Be organized.
6. Say "yes, sir" and "yes, ma'am" to other adults.

2. Disciple, More Than Just an Eight Letter Word (Have a set plan for discipling new Christians)

One of the big buzz words is "accountability". But that is not all that discipling is to be. If I were going to make someone a disciple of basketball, I would first teach them about the game. Then train them to play the game. Then equip them with the tools to get better. Accountability is not the end step, but rather a part of each step.

Teach them what leadership is. Leadership is not doing all the work. It is working with a team to finish the job. Leadership is not telling everyone what to do. Leadership is showing everyone what to do. Leadership is not moving people. Leadership is motivating people to movement. One of my favorite quotes is by an anonymous writer. "He who leads without followers is merely taking a walk." Many student leaders fail because they have a wrong or incomplete view of leadership. Jesus modeled true leadership for us. He taught 12 guys what leading was, how to do it, and then He left them with the tools to lead. To the Pharisees, leading was controlling people. To Jesus, leading was helping, directing, and serving people. Leadership is not being served but rather serving.

Train them to lead. There are so many different leadership styles but the most successful leaders employ three tactics:

1. Define what the purpose of the task or project is.
2. Develop a plan that accomplishes your purpose.
3. Recruit people to fill every position and task.

In light of training a young person to lead, defining the purpose of the task can not be overstated. We can all become wrapped up in packaging and details and miss the big picture. So a very clear presentation of purpose must come first and generally be revisited.

Developing the plan is where discipling really comes into play. You have to help them think about things they do not envision. Recruiting other students and adults who can do what the student leaders cannot, can sometimes be intimidating. Knowing how to place and employ people is strength and not weakness.

Equipping means to give them the resources. It could involve showing them how to use software or taking them to a conference. Giving your leader the right tools will only help them be effective and successful. Not giving them the needed tools will mean inefficiency and frustration. Now, with all this said, let's take a project and walk through how we could teach, train, and equip a student or adult to lead.

Project: Super Bowl Party

1. Have a face-to-face meeting with your proposed leader where you share your purpose for this Super Bowl party.
2. Give them the budget for the party.
3. Brainstorm ideas for the party with a few students or a team of students.

Super Bowl Bash Plan

3 Months Out
- Pray about a team leader
- Set up meetings with prospective Team Leaders
- Choose a Team Leader
- Secure a place for event

6 Weeks Out
- Meet with team leader and share vision
  (This year we want the Super Bowl Party to accomplish two major things: bring in lost students and secondly to be a community building event among our students)
- Give the budget
- Dream about ideas for the event
- Ask Team Leader to assemble a Core Team to lead each aspect (Give-A-Ways, Registration, Technical, Food, Parking, Security, Publicity, Gospel presentation, etc.)

5 Weeks Out
- Follow up with Team Leader about Core Team members
- Begin announcements
- Have lunch with publicity team leader to work on publicity plan
- Secure any rentals (inflatable toys, popcorn machine, etc.)
- Decide who is doing the halftime event
- Decide beginning and ending time
- Work on theme for the night

4 Weeks Out
- Put up posters and flyers at schools, clubs, etc.
- Send out postcards to your students
- Meet with Core Team leaders to discuss each facet of event
- Recruit extra adults
- Petition for door prizes

3 Weeks Out
- Begin radio announcements
- Go over menu with Food Core Team leader
- Layout event in the actual place it will be held

2 Weeks Out
- Begin collecting door prizes
- Confirm with all rental places

Week Of
- Institute prayer chain
- Last meeting with Team Leader and Core Team
- Set up for event

3. It's a Memory Game! (Memorize scripture with them)

It can be very difficult and will definitely be time consuming but will offer great rewards. There is something marvelous that happens when you challenge your leaders to memorize God's Word with you. It seems to unify you as a team and really helps them to see God's Word in a different light.

You can memorize a verse a week, a section of verses a semester, or a certain section for mission trips. There are many ways to package it. The important thing is to do it!

4. My House is Your House (Spend time with them in your home)

Part of discipling leadership means to train and teach, but there is a facet that can only be done by spending quality time together. The family concept not only affects the community of your group but the health of your leaders. Having student and adult leaders in your home transcends the classroom atmosphere and builds trust. It is a chance for you to example how to act away from "church" and an opportunity for them to see you work behind the scenes.

There are three times we invite leaders into our home. The first is when we are teaming up to plan and work on a big event. The general feel of a meeting is more relaxed in our living room. Secondly, we invite leaders into our home for special parties to celebrate or commemorate events. Christmas, end of school, graduation, and after a big youth event are all times to have special parties. Thirdly, we have leaders in our home for "hang-out" time. Thursday night each week at 7pm our student leaders are welcome at the Hudson's. Sometimes we play games, sometimes we watch a special presentation on TV, and other times we discuss serious or light hearted questions that are relative to what they have faced that day at school or at home.

5. Road Trip 1 (Take them to conferences with you)

There is a special something that happens when you spend quality time in dreaming, vision casting, and planning with your leadership students. At a conference is a great place to do just that. So what do you want to accomplish at a conference? Making my top ten list of reasons to go to a conference would be, and not necessarily in this order:

10. To spend time with other pastors and people who share your passion for reaching students.
9. To hear the latest music.
8. To gain a new perspective on youth ministry by seeing what programs, studies, and events other people are doing successfully in their ministries.
7. To be refreshed.
6. To catch up with old friends.
5. To get away from the grind.
4. To learn how other people exercise creativity.
3. To be led in the kind of worship you lead each week.
2. To have time with your leaders.
1. Eating out.

So where do your students fit in? Well, not that you would want to take them with you every time, but there is some value in strategically taking a handful of leadership students and adult leaders to conferences. So what do you do with them? Build community with them by sitting together in the main sessions and make them feel a part of the team by sending them to individual sessions and making them responsible for taking notes. As a team, walk around the facilities and take notes on building layout, creative aspects, and the things that wow you. Eat your meals together and then that night back in the hotel spend time brainstorming and sharing notes from that day's sessions.

6. Road Trip 2 (Take them with you to speaking engagements)

Most students need to see an example more often and before they hear the lecture. When you take a student leader with you to speak at a youth revival, Disciple Now, or FCA meeting, make sure you follow 4 simple rules.

1. Study and be prepared.
2. Treat every adult there with respect.
3. Always be humble and thankful for any food and every gift or compliment.
4. Be on time.

What you are doing is investing in the future, yours and theirs. To have students see how you handle unique situations is a bonus. What you will find is that not all of your leadership students will become pastors but they will stay leaders. They will look to you for how to respond to sticky situations. Here is a short list of some peculiar opportunities I have found myself in while trying to lead by example for my leadership students.

- Had a special needs student (mentally handicapped) try to consume my time.
- Altar call in a different place.
- An angry parent.

I'm sure there are others and for me, will be more. The fact is your students can learn from you not only when things are working like a well-oiled machine, but also when things fall apart. Do your best to be a leader in all situations.

7. Your Turn! (Give them opportunities to speak, lead, or direct)

Investing all sorts of training in your students and taking them with you on trips is of no value if you never give them a chance to practice what they have learned. Opportunity is the key to leadership for a student. He or she can know what to do in their head but until they have been placed in a unique situation, they will not understand completely what it is to lead. Look for places in your ministry where you can give pieces and hunks of responsibility over to your student leaders. Listed below are a few things to keep in mind when empowering your student leaders.

1. Let them do it, even if it is not the way you would do it. They will learn more from their own failure than from your saving them.
2. Help them set goals. When you give them a leadership task, without a goal they will aimlessly wander. However, make the goals attainable taking into consideration their maturity, schedule, and ability.
3. Help them be accountable. Not only will they work better with an objective, but knowing you are going to call them to task on their progress will prove a viable initiator for them.
4. Give them the credit. Make sure you applaud their efforts in front of the students, their parents, the pastor, and who ever else will listen. They will know where they goofed; help remind them of what they did great.

So where do you start? How much do you give away? The following is a list of some possible starting points.

1. A three minute devotional or testimony
2. Organize a "Thank You" event for adult workers
3. Welcome and opening for youth event or program
4. Organize greeters for Sunday morning
5. Host snacks for a parent meeting
6. Deliver visitor gifts to homes
7. Lead music for praise band
8. Lead student orchestra
9. Give announcements in a large group setting
10. Make them the contact person for an event

Just remember to set up achievable goals and proper accountability. You will begin to see students rise to the challenge. Paul exhorted us that our job is to "equip the saints for the work of the ministry". (Ephesians 4:12) When you do this, be encouraged. This is a process of "equipping them for the work of ministry". This process will require extra work and added investment into the personal lives of those student leaders. But it is what we are called and commanded to do . . . making disciples, equipping saints!

Blueprint #8

To Connect with Visitors

To Connect with Visitors
1. The Three Levels of "Hello" (Make connections with people)
2. The Hook (Get their info on a youth visitor card)
3. Doggy Bag . . . take it home and gnaw on it
4. Here's Your Sign (Put up yard signs)
5. Set It and Forget It! (Have a planned outreach time)

It doesn't take long in a mall to see that there is an array of ways to advertise ourselves. But the question that is answered with every style is "Who?" Why does JC Penny's look and even feel differ from the Gap? They are different because they are reaching a different audience. Inside of each visitor is an undefined fear of the unknown. From the most socially introverted to the captain of the cheer squad, the unknown can be scary and intimidating. Our goal is to make visitors feel comfortable so they can determine if this is the family for them. We want them to think, "I can see myself fitting in here."

There are five students who God allows to step through your doors. The first is the unsaved teen who has followed a friend or been pushed by a circumstance. They are looking for the Jesus in you and your family and most likely, if they receive Him at your church, they will stay at your church to be a member of the family. The second is the Christian student who has no loyalty to any membership and is looking for a good experience more than a God experience. The third is the Christian young person who has wandered away from church all together and in time has found themselves wanting, needing something but not knowing what that something is. That something is the desire to fellowship with other Christians and to be a part of a family that provides an experience bigger than themselves. The fourth kind of student is the Christian who is new in town or searching for a new church home. And the fifth is the out-of-towner, in for the weekend at Grandma and Grandpa's house. With the first four students in mind there is a process in which teens enter and exit our ministries.

1. Invitation – They are given an invitation by a friend or family member. It is the carrot that dangles in front of the horse so to speak. The more personal the invitation, the more open the student is to the experience.

2. First Impression – Knowing that each student will develop an initial concept of your youth group within the first 3 minutes of setting foot in your church makes a difference. You will spend the rest of your time either confirming that student's original ideas or desperately trying to convince them otherwise.

3. Assimilation – A good first impression needs to be followed up with answering the question, "Where do I fit in here?" Assimilation, how you plug that student into your youth group and the other students will determine the longevity of that student in your ministry.

Before they can get to the point where they understand who we are and what our ministries are about, we must gain their confidence.

1. The Three Levels of "Hello" (Make connections with people)

Here is the scene. It is a Sunday morning and a student who is visiting Grandma has been told all about your student ministry. Grandma has read about your activities in the bulletin, seen the students doing service projects, and has even heard you preach a time or two. Grandma is convinced that little Tommy or Suzie will enjoy spending an hour with you and your group in Bible study. Little Tommy or Suzie on the other hand are at best, hesitant. They don't know anyone, they don't know what you have planned, and most of the time they are there to please Grandma. As Tommy or Suzie step into the door of your youth room or building, what is their first thought? Where do I go from here? They need someone to talk to them, to show them where to go, and what to do. This is where the three levels of "Hello" come in. The three levels are:

1. Hello from a door greeter.
2. Hello from you the student pastor or leader.
3. Hello from a welcome team.

First, there should be someone at your entrance to welcome students. It can be a student or an adult but they need to be familiar with who are members so they can easily recognize visitors. Door Greeters are your first line of offense. They are your first impression on people and need to be smiling, contagiously happy, and able to communicate. Often times a 14 year-old student can handle the first two factors but bomb on the third. All three factors are important. A smile is what the student sees before he or she ever hears a word. A smile will set the tone for what you are about to say. Your contagious joy will be reflected in your speech and give a visitor the assurance that you are glad to be there and they should be glad to be there, too. The third factor, the ability to communicate, gives the visitor confidence that they are going to be taken care of and that they can relax.

So what does the Door Greeter communicate? The Door Greeter's job is to communicate confidence while at the same time getting vital information without sounding like they are interrogating the visitor.

Good morning. (with expression and inflection in your voice) How are you? You look like you might be a visitor today. My name is _____. What is your name? Well, _____, are you here with your family? (Whether they have come by themselves or with a friend or family the answer is . . .) Great! _____, we are so glad you are here. _____, I would like to introduce you to our student pastor, Paul. He would love to know you are here.

Notice that once the door greeter gets the student's name they use their name throughout the conversation. This builds confidence and eases nervousness of the visitor.

Then comes handoff one – from the door greeter to the student pastor or leader.

The door greeter walks the visitor over to the student pastor (who is standing near the same spot to talk to students each event). He/She gets the student pastor's attention and introduces the visitor to him.

Paul, I would like to introduce _____ to you. He/She is here today with _____.

To which the student pastor replies:

Thanks, _____. Hello _____, it is so nice to meet you and I am so glad you are here. How old are you? What school do you attend? Do you like sports? Do you play an instrument? How long have you been playing? *(You don't have to use all these questions. The idea is to find out something about the student so you can better know who you can put them with.)* Great! Do you know anyone here? Well let's go find a couple of students who will hang out with you and show you the ropes today.

Then you pick up a visitor card (we will talk about that next) and head together to go find a couple of students. Hand off number two.

You should find students in your group who have the ability to talk easily with other students. Train them on how to start conversations and to keep it going. Example for them the way to smile, to be contagiously happy, and to communicate. The purpose of this welcome team is to get that visitor through the next hour. The welcome team should let the visitor know what is going to happen during the service and invite the visitor to sit with them. They should also be able to help the visitor fill out a visitor card and answer questions about other programs and events in the youth group.

Choosing a welcome team:
1. Choose people who want to be on the welcome team.

2. Choose people who are consistent in their attendance.
3. Choose people from each age group or study group you have.
4. Choose people who have positive attitudes.

By using the three levels of "Hello", visitors see people and build relationships instead of seeing buildings or programs. And students will come back because of a relationship more than they will because of a cool room or fun program. Students will size up your program or ministry within the first three minutes. The three levels of "Hello" allow you to connect with a visitor while they are forming that first impression about your ministry rather than you having to go back and try to explain yourself over a preconceived opinion.

2. The Hook (Get their info on a youth visitor card)

Once a student steps foot in your youth room, the biggest hook you have to get them back again, besides the relationships they build with students, will be getting their contact information. Whether you call it a Guest Student Information Card, Visitors Card, or the Blue Card, get the necessary information you need to be able to follow up on them with a phone call and a home visit.

Try to make the card as appealing as possible and easy to follow. A student who is unfamiliar with you and your ministry will only fill out what he or she easily understands. So use multiple-choice and have few blanks. Have a set place where they turn the card in to a person. The personal contact of handing that card to another human being is vital. When they look another student or a caring adult in the face and hear, "Thank you for coming. We hope you had a good time and will come back next week" it carries more weight. In the days to follow, it will be harder to forget the face of that person than it would be to forget the color of the table you had them set the card on.

So what do you need to know?
- Their name, address, phone, email
- Birthday, age, grade in school, which school
- Who they have come with
- Which event or program they came to and the date

Just a few more thoughts about visitor cards.
1. Don't have them fill out a card during your program. They will give you half information because they want to see what is going on next.
2. No matter how you get the information, have them turn it in or communicate it to a person. That makes another connection.

3. Doggy Bag . . . take it home and gnaw on it

The idea of a Doggy Bag came after a trip to one of our town's nicer restaurants. When it came time to check out, the waiter asked if we would like a Doggy Bag, so we could take it home with us. The idea stuck and hence we started giving out Doggy Bags to visitors. A simple and inexpensive gift can go a long way to impressing a guest and making a connection. **What** you give is as important as the fact that you **do** give. Here are a few ideas of things we put in our Doggy Bags.
-   T-shirts from past events or Bible study series
-   Refrigerator magnets with youth group logo, web site, and phone number
-   Candy
-   Simple, colorful brochure about our programs
-   Wristband with youth group logo
-   Can of Pepsi or Coke
-   Youth calendar or monthly newsletter
-   Left over promo materials
-   Thank you note (for coming)

Make sure you have the youth group contact info somewhere in there.

What Bag?

Brown paper bags with handles are always good because they are neutral. You can print a Doggie Bag label on sticky paper to put on the bag with your logo and initial information and you are ready to surprise a visitor. You can also try getting the colored bags at a local specialty store. You can even have bags printed at a printer. Whatever you use, the idea is to get a bag and a label that are easily recognizable for your students. You want a bag that is big enough to fit all your stuff in but not so big that it seems half full.

4. Here's Your Sign (Put up yard signs)

This is one of those fun things that you almost feel sneaky about. Simply put "Thanks" signs up in the yards of students who are visiting. You can do this a couple different ways but the effect is the same . . . they love it.

The Sign

You want a sign that is relatively small; about the size of a political campaign sign or smaller. It needs to be printed on a heavy card stock. If you cannot afford to have them printed like this, you can print on a full sheet label and then stick it to cardboard. Try to keep the text simple and to the point. Your youth group logo with the word "Thanks!" usually will suffice.

How to set it up

You will need a wooden stake, a heavy duty stapler, and a hammer. Experience has taught us to hammer the stake into the ground first, and then staple the sign onto the wooden stake.

Where to set it up

Place the sign in the front yard where it can be seen from the road and/or the driveway. Be sure and put it away from the street but not too close to the house.

When to set it up

You need to find what works for you but here are three ways to do signs.

1. If you have the people power, have someone go out while the student is actually at your event or service and put it up in their yard. When they get home, it is already there waiting on them. This is very impressive to parents.
2. If you have a person who would commit to taking care of this as a ministry, you can give this task to them each week. Let them pick a day each week that they could get the visitor list from you and go out on sign mission.
3. Have your students do it as another part of your outreach program. This is a good way to break up phone calls and house visits.

It is also a good idea to attach a couple of letters to the back side of the sign. The first letter labeled "Parents" that is a basic "thank you" to the parents for allowing them to come to your church. The second letter is to the student thanking them as well. In the student letter you can also put coupons for drinks or desserts from around town.

5. Set It and Forget It! (Have a planned outreach time)

Outreach is one of those concepts under dispute for many student pastors. In an age where parents and kids alike are so driven by sports, it is easier to catch them at the ball park. And I certainly think if we are going to stay relative and relational with our students, we have to make time in our schedule for games and recitals. However, there is no substitute for meeting with a student and/or their parent at their home, on their turf. Most parents will not only appreciate that you have taken time to come to their house, they will turn off the TV and internet and sit down with their student to talk to you. There is recognition of special attention that a student has when you go to their house and visit them on their terms.

A good outreach plan should consider three questions:

1. Who needs to be contacted?
2. How will they be contacted?

3. Who is going to contact them?

Who needs to be contacted?

Visitors, non-active members, and active members . . . wait a minute, that is everyone!? That's right. The fact is every person in your ministry needs to be contacted on a regular basis. Whether by their small group leader, another student, or you, each one needs that personal contact that lets them know they are important and connected.

Visitors need to be contacted immediately. Members who have missed an event should be contacted that week. Active members should be contacted monthly. There will be those students who fall out of your ministry as fast as they fell into it. You have to know when to let them go or encourage them to attend another ministry. But for the most part, keep in personal touch with every student monthly.

How will they be contacted?

There is a plethora, yes that means a bunch, of ways you can employ to stay connected and contacted to your students. The trick is to find what works for your students and for you. Consider time, cost, and comprehension. Time: is this feasible for me to do this for each person in the group? Cost: can I afford this in my budget? Comprehension: will the student understand and appreciate this form of communication?

As a general rule, never put rebuke or negative words in print. Use the following forms of communication as encouragement and building relationships. Save any rebuke or correcting you need to do for a face-to-face visit.

Personal Notes (Scheduled outreach or office time)

For years this has been my best plan for a personal contact outside home visits. In a world of faxes, emails, and instant messaging, there is something special about a short handwritten note. It communicates sincerity and on a certain level a degree to friendship. Whether you use a stock stationery of your own or of the churches, use white paper from the copy room, or get nice stationery, the effort will be appreciated and rewarded.

Email

Although not my first choice, a close second is email and instant messaging. We live in a time where every student is more computer savvy than the group two years their senior. They are not only living for computers, they are living on their computers. Utilize both personal emails and bulk emails. Try to limit the bulk emails to your students to information and always save relational conversations for personal emails. Along this line of thought, you can try opening a chat room on your youth group web page.

Message on tape, CD, or DVD

This will take some effort and a little know how, but with the right stuff, you can easily record personalized letters to your students on tape, CD, or DVD. I started mailing "Paul-O-Grams" years ago as one of those one-time leaps in the dark at creativity, and it worked! You have to do what works for you, but I simply hit record and begin talking to the student as if they were sitting in my office.

Phone Calls

During regularly scheduled outreach times, employ students who are new or bashful to make phone calls. The following is a list of who to call and why.
- Call visitors to thank them for coming (Always call them by name)
- Call active members to remind them of special outreach events
- Call everyone on your roll to remind them about special upcoming events

- Call small group absentees to tell them they were missed that week

Before unleashing a group of well-meaning absent minded students to calling all over town in the name of your church, take time to train them on phone etiquette. If need be, give them a simple script to help them stay on target and remember simple rules of politeness.

Home Visits

In our culture, people now consider their home their castle. Fifteen years ago, people considered their homes places of interaction and looked for hosting opportunities. To invite someone into their home was a privilege. Today, thanks to busy schedules and hectic life styles, homes are more like fortified refuges set up with invisible but understood boundaries. Follow these 6 simple rules to home visits and not only will your visits be successful, you will be invited back.

1. **Always call before you show up.** We call visitors they day they visit and thank them for coming or the next day. Our initial conversation lets them know we do student outreach on Monday nights and we ask if they would like for someone to stop by and answer questions or explain details of programs to their student. Then we call about two hours before we make the visit to remind the student and family we are coming.

2. **Be on time.** If you have gone to the effort to let the family know when you will be there, don't keep them. It shows you respect their time and are a person of your word.

3. **Don't stay too long but don't hurry off.** If it is a visitor or prospect, simply introduce yourself and the student with you, give them some printed information, and give them a quick overview. Explain to them in a few words your purpose, your passion, and your plans and then get out. If it is a member, encourage them, pray with them, and bug. However, you should not try to rush your conversation, just don't let it drag on and on.

4. **Respect their property.** Usually, really expensive houses have really expensive things in them. Take students who can maintain

a cordial level of civility and then example for them what to do. If shoes are sitting by the door that is a good clue that you should take yours off before stepping onto the carpet. If you are given a drink, only set your cup or glass on a coaster. Simple rules of etiquette can keep you from embarrassing yourself and losing the confidence of a visitor.

5. **Leave them something.** Whether it is a CD or DVD about your youth group, a printed brochure about an upcoming event, or your business card, leave them with something they can put their hands on.

6. **Allow them to talk.** Try to ask questions that will help you find out about their interests and hobbies. Asking the right questions can tell you a lot about their spiritual depth, their level of commitment, and their interest in your youth program. If they go off on some story, let them talk.

7. **Pray with them.** No matter if the visit has been pleasant or less than stellar, just about every person you encounter will allow you to pray for them. Of course your tone and demeanor can play a helpful role in this, but give it a try. As you are getting ready to leave, try this:

Mr. Jones and Leslie, thank you all so much for your time tonight. Rachel and I know you are very busy but before we go, is there anything we can pray for you all about? Any special need we can ask God to meet?

Almost every time you will find this to be an open door. With earnestness and joy, pray with them.

Blueprint #9

To Grow Respect

To Grow Respect
1. Live Out What You Teach (Movies, music, etc.)
2. Let's Pray (Pray for your Pastor and staff regularly)
3. Know What You're Doing! (Be prepared for Bible study)
4. Your Word is Your Bond (Do what you say you will do)

Student pastors tend to struggle with the concept of being 'grown up" enough to be a minister and earn the respect of parents, pastors, and community members while at the same time being "cool" enough to stay in tune with their students.

There are two myths that tend to pull respect away from the youth pastor position. The first is that we are working our way up to something else. It is true that many pastors got their humble beginnings in church work as youth pastors. For some reason it is the place where we take the most impressionable group of people and hand them over to the most inexperienced person and expect the most exciting results. If you are in student ministry, it should be because you are called and not because you need to pad a resume. If God puts you there and then moves you on, that is fine. God is God and He can lead and direct in His economy. But in general, way too many youth pastors are in the ministry Bermuda triangle waiting to be found for their dream job or ministry. In the meantime a generation of spiritually starving young adults is making choices that will affect the rest of their lives and eternity.

Several years ago a family member, by marriage and of another religion, asked me one Christmas, "So Paul, how is church work these days?" I replied, "Things are great and God is good!" His next question made me laugh . . . out-loud, and then I had to apologize because I realized he was serious. "Do you hope to work your way up to Pastor any time soon?" Work my way up?! I am a student pastor because God told me to be, not because it is the bottom of the pastor rung.

The other myth that tends to steal respect is that student pastors just play with the kids. This can be accentuated when the student pastor is a young guy and inexperienced in creating and planning Bible studies. The natural thing is to fill our inadequacy with something we are good at . . . playing around. No matter what your style or ability in teaching, if you will exercise great amounts of energy in preparing Biblically based life-applicable studies that are both creative and on target, you will find your students thirsting for more. You will earn respect from your students and they will listen as you talk. Parents will begin to take you more seriously. And your pastor, well, cut him some slack because for most of you he is 25 years your senior.

1. Live Out What You Teach (Movies, music, etc.)

Sometimes our biggest enemies are our own actions. They really do speak louder than words. We don't have respect from our students because we don't earn respect. Students are more likely to remember our actions much longer than the witty words of encouragement or constructive criticism we tend to offer in eloquent bits and pieces of sarcastic review. To students, we are operating in a sphere they don't comprehend. Married people, who can stay up as late as they want, spend their money how they want, and who have lots of money (at least in their eyes), are telling them they should wait to have sex, be respectful to their parents, give part of their money to God, and not waste their lives. Try as you may, your theologically profound Bible studies relating the human condition to a common household item or the building of a brick house will not connect unless they get it, catch it, grasp it, and understand it. And to do all those things they have to see it lived out in your life. Basically, if you draw a line in the sand for them, be willing to stand behind it yourself.

There are four areas a student pastor really needs to example moral and spiritual maturity for their students.

1. Movies. We don't watch any rated "R" movies; none! End of discussion. Is it because we can't handle the violence, sex, and language? To us, we don't want to handle it. 1 Tim 2:22 says to flee evil desires. We will only watch PG and PG-13 movies (not even all of those) and have found the best thing to do is to wait until something comes on TV or to use the TV guardian. Many of our students have parents who tell them not to watch bad stuff but then allow them to watch movies with sexually explicit and verbally vulgar scenes that stain and corrupt their minds. Be strong not only for the students but for their parents also.

2. Music. Yes, you knew it was coming. I am one of those proponents of Christian music only. Why? The long answer is another time and another book. The short answer is Philippians 4:8. "Whatsoever things are kind, lovely, pure, good, and of good report, think on these things." The number one answer I get is "I don't listen to the words." We all know that isn't true. My five year old daughter knows better than that. As she screams and sings every word to Super Chick ask her if she only hears the music. And if they are getting the words, the words are taking root and creating thoughts. Thoughts lead to actions, actions to habits. Habits to character and I think you get my drift. The second answer I get is "Paul, this song isn't bad and doesn't have any cuss words or talk about anything bad." To which I usually ask the question, "Is God true because the Bible says He is? Or is the Bible true because God says it is?" The Bible is true because God said. Whether the Bible was here or not God is still real and true. If God were not here, the Bible would be of no affect. It is the source. And in their music, is the source a person who loves and fears God? Or is it a person who has been given over to a perverse and depraved mind like Romans 1 talks about?

3. Obedience to authorities. As you show respect to your elders, your students will begin to see the benefits and joy of giving respect to you. Let's say you go to a school campus for lunch and as some of your students enter the lunch room they are complaining about a teacher. You don't have to defend the teacher because you don't really know what happened. But you can encourage your students to respect that teacher's authority and see where God's hand is in the big picture. 1 Peter says we are to show "proper respect" to worldly authorities and in turn we please God and respect Him.

4. Clothing. What you wear, your spouse wears, and what you allow the students to wear around you will also shape their respect for you. If you set a standard with students, be ready to abide by it in every area of your life. A good thought with respect to what we wear would be that if what you are wearing draws attention to anywhere other than your face, it will draw the wrong kind of attention. We could spend hours on this one subject but will leave this to another book and another time. Just beware, the eyes are the window to your mind and heart; guard them well!

2. Let's Pray (Pray for your Pastor and staff regularly)

It is no secret that the greatest of great nations, businesses, and people are destroyed from within. As a family member of your church, you have a responsibility and a privilege to pray for your Pastor and staff.

The responsibility comes from a scriptural mandate to "pray for each other" (James 5:16). It is not a legalistic view of offering up half hearted requests or petitions for some name on a list. It is a sincere communication between you and your heavenly Father in which you ask the Creator of the Universe to be involved in a very real and personal way.

The privilege side of praying for your Pastor and staff comes because you love them and know that God hears your prayers. It is wonderful to be able to "carry each other's burdens" (Gal 6:2) in prayer to God. Praying for them makes you mindful of other aspects of your church and will cause you to see your church from a different perspective. As you make it a habit of praying for your fellow staff members, it becomes very natural to pray for them while in front of your youth. Before long, they sense the tender heart and camaraderie you have with the other staff and find themselves wanting to pray for you.

The greatest way to get your students to pray for you is to lead by example and pray for your leaders. Be careful not to pray like the Pharisee or like Gossiping Gail. Simply "by prayer and petition, with thanksgiving, present your requests to God." (Phil 4:6) Your students are smart enough to pick up on ulterior motives in your prayers. So follow these four simple steps to praying for your Pastor and staff.

1. Talk to God and not the students in your prayers.
2. Mention them by their name.
3. Ask God to give them wisdom and understanding in leadership.
4. Thank God for their positive qualities and call them out.

3. Know What You're Doing! (Be prepared for Bible study)

If there was one area of a student pastor's ministry that will cause him to loose the respect of parents and their students the quickest, it would be in their preparation and delivery of Bible studies. So many times we put hours of effort into set design, music, games, and our demonstrations and leave 10 minutes to study God's Word and to decide what we will say. Chapter Five (How to Prepare Bible Studies) covered this topic in depth. Understand that you have been called to feed your students before you have been called to play with them or entertain them. (John 21:15) Simply put, feed His sheep! Feed His sheep! Feed His Sheep!

4. Your Word is Your Bond (Do what you say you will do)

Every student pastor wants to be involved in the lives of the students they work with. It is not only a joy but also a vital part of ministering to them. However, the desire to be involved coupled with their asking you to be involved can at times cause us to make commitments that we can't physically keep. There are times that the desire to meet needs and accomplish the daily tasks of being a student pastor just can't be fit in to one day. Often we tell students we will be at a game or visit them at lunch and wind up missing. They feel bad, we feel bad, and it's just . . . bad. So how do we make sure that we earn and keep a student's respect? By doing what we say we will do. It sounds simple, but the concept is novel, ***think before you speak***. Once you have told a student you will visit them, your word is your bond. Do everything you can to visit them. In a case where you have to break that word because of unforeseen circumstances, call them and let them know. Never just skip out on them. If you can't be at a game, recital, play, or lunch, don't tell them you will.

Once you are with a student or group of students, do your best to give them your full attention. If you stack your appointments up so that you only have 15 minutes at the JV basketball game and then have to swing over to make a home visit, then back to the church for a meeting you **will** miss something. You will also make every person you deal with feel like you don't have time for them. Carry a calendar so that you can know your schedule and only commit to what you can *actually* do.

Bottom line . . .
- Be where you say you will be.
- Do what you say you will do.
- Go where you say you will go.

Having the respect of your students and their parents is necessary. Without respect you will never be able to lead. Don't confuse "like" with "respect". If you are leading well and demanding respect then there will certainly be times when you are disliked. But that will come and go. Be consistent.

Conclusion

Student ministry is for the strong of heart and courageous of spirit. As a leader of young adults you possess the privilege and the responsibility to impact a generation for Christ. You hold the keys to unlocking true life for young men and women—an authentic relationship with Jesus Christ. The old cliché says it well. Keep the main thing the main thing. As you act justly, love mercy, and walk humbly with God (Micah 6:8) you will live out an example that will speak much louder than your words.

"He has showed you, O man, what is good. And what does the Lord require of you? To act justly and to love mercy and to walk humbly with your God." Micah 6:8